# BOOMERANG

**Center Point
Large Print**

**This Large Print Book carries the
Seal of Approval of N.A.V.H.**

# BOOMERANG

Travels in the New Third World

# Michael Lewis

CENTER POINT PUBLISHING
THORNDIKE, MAINE

This Center Point Large Print edition
is published in the year 2011 by arrangement with
W. W. Norton & Co., Inc.

Grateful acknowledgment is made to *Vanity Fair*,
where the pieces in this book appeared, in slightly
different form: "Wall Street on the Tundra," April 2009;
"Beware of Greeks Bearing Bonds," October 2010;
"When Irish Eyes Are Crying," March 2011;
"It's the Economy, Dummkopf!," September 2011;
"Too Fat to Fly," November 2011.

The text of this Large Print edition is unabridged.
In other aspects, this book may vary
from the original edition.
Printed in the United States of America
on permanent paper.
Set in 16-point Times New Roman type.

ISBN: 978-1-61173-252-8

Library of Congress Cataloging-in-Publication Data

Lewis, Michael (Michael M.)
Boomerang : travels in the new third world / Michael Lewis.
p. cm.
Originally published : New York : W. W. Norton & Co., 2011.
ISBN 978-1-61173-252-8 (library binding : alk. paper)
1. Global Financial Crisis, 2008–2009. 2. International finance.
   3. Financial crises—United States—History—21st century. I. Title.
HB37172008 .L49 2011b
330.9´0511—dc23

2011032198

To Doug Stumpf, gifted editor and gentle soul, without whom it never would have occurred to me to tour the ruins

# CONTENTS

# PREFACE

## THE BIGGEST SHORT

This book began accidentally, while I was at work on another book, about Wall Street and the 2008 U.S. financial disaster. I'd become interested in a tiny handful of investors who had made their fortunes from the collapse of the subprime mortgage market. Back in 2004, the biggest Wall Street investment banks had created the instrument of their own destruction, the credit default swap on the subprime mortgage bond. The credit default swap enabled investors to bet against the price of any given bond—to "short" it. It was an insurance policy, but with a twist: the buyer didn't need to own the insured asset. No insurance company can legally sell you fire protection on another person's house, but the financial markets can and will sell you default insurance on another person's investments. Hundreds of investors had dabbled in the credit default swap market—a lot of people had thought, at least in passing, that the debt-fueled U.S. housing boom was unsustainable—but only fifteen or so had gone all in, and placed enormous bets that vast tracts of American finance would go up in flames. Most of these people ran hedge funds in London or New York; most, usually, avoided journalists. But on this topic, at this moment, they were surprisingly open. All had experienced the strange and isolating sensation of being the sane man in an insane world and, when they talked about their experience, sounded as a person might if he had sat alone and in silence in a small boat and watched the *Titanic* steam into the iceberg.

A few of these people were temperamentally ill-suited to solitude and silence. Among this subset was the manager of a hedge fund called Hayman Capital, in Dallas, Texas. His name was Kyle Bass. Bass was a native Texan in his late thirties who had spent the first years of his career, seven of them at Bear Stearns, selling bonds for Wall Street firms. In late 2006 he'd taken half of the $10 million he had saved from his Wall Street career, raised another $500 million from other people, created his hedge fund, and made a massive wager against the subprime mortgage bond market. Then he'd flown to New York to warn his old friends that they were on the wrong side of a lot of stupid bets. The traders at Bear Stearns had no interest in what he had to say. "You worry about your risk management. I'll worry about ours," one of them had told him. By the end of 2008, when I went to Dallas to see Bass, the subprime mortgage bond market had collapsed, taking Bear Stearns with it. He was now rich and even, in investment circles, a little famous. But his mind had moved on from the subprime mortgage bond debacle: having taken his profits, he had a new all-consuming interest, governments. The United States government was just then busy taking on to its own books the subprime loans made by Bear Stearns and other Wall Street banks. The Federal Reserve would wind up absorbing the risk, in one form or another, associated with nearly $2 trillion in dodgy securities. Its actions were of a piece with those of other governments in the rich, developed world: the bad loans made by highly paid financiers working in the private sector were being eaten by national treasuries and central banks everywhere.

In Kyle Bass's opinion, the financial crisis wasn't over. It was simply being smothered by the full faith and credit of rich Western governments. I spent a day listening to him and his colleagues discuss, almost giddily, where this might lead. They were no longer talking about the collapse of a few bonds. They were talking about the collapse of entire countries.

And they had a shiny new investment thesis. It ran, roughly, as follows. From 2002 there had been something like a false boom in much of the rich, developed world. What appeared to be economic growth was activity fueled by people borrowing money they probably couldn't afford to repay: by their rough count, worldwide debts, public and private, had more than doubled since 2002, from $84 trillion to $195 trillion. "We've never had this kind of accumulation of debt in world history," said Bass. Critically, the big banks that had extended much of this credit were no longer treated as private enterprises but as extensions of their local governments, sure to be bailed out in a crisis. The public debt of rich countries already stood at what appeared to be dangerously high levels and, in response to the crisis, was rapidly growing. But the public debt of these countries was no longer the official public debt. As a practical matter it included the debts inside each country's banking system, which, in another crisis, would be transferred to the government. "The first thing we tried to figure out," said Bass, "was how big these banking systems were, especially in relation to government revenues. We took about four months to gather the data. No one had it."

The numbers added up to astonishing totals: Ireland, for instance, with its large and growing annual deficits, had amassed debts of more than twenty-five times its annual tax revenues. Spain and France had accumulated debts of more than ten times their annual revenues. Historically, such levels of government indebtedness had led to government default. "Here's the only way I think things can work out for these countries," Bass said. "If they start running real budget surpluses. Yeah, and that will happen right after *monkeys fly out of your ass.*"

Still, he wondered if perhaps he was missing something. "I went looking for someone, anyone, who knew something about the history of sovereign defaults," he said. He found the leading expert on the subject, a professor at Harvard named Kenneth Rogoff, who, as it happened, was preparing a book on the history of national financial collapse, *This Time Is Different: Eight Centuries of Financial Folly*, with fellow scholar Carmen Reinhart. "We walked Rogoff through the numbers," said Bass, "and he just looked at them, then sat back in his chair, and said, 'I can hardly believe it is this bad.' And I said, 'Wait a minute. You're the world's foremost expert on sovereign balance sheets. You are the go-to guy for sovereign trouble. You taught at Princeton with Ben Bernanke. You introduced Larry Summers to his second wife. If you don't know this, who does?' I thought, Holy shit, who is paying attention?"

Thus his new investment thesis: the subprime mortgage crisis was more symptom than cause. The deeper social and economic problems that gave rise to it remained. The moment that investors woke up to this reality, they would cease to think of big Western governments as essentially risk-free and demand higher rates of interest to lend to them. When the interest rates on their borrowing rose, these governments would plunge further into debt, leading to further rises in the interest rates they were charged to borrow. In a few especially alarming cases— Greece, Ireland, Japan—it wouldn't take much of a rise in interest rates for budgets to be consumed entirely by interest payments on debt. "For example," said Bass, "if Japan had to borrow at France's rates, the interest burden alone would bankrupt the government." The moment the financial markets realized this, investor sentiment would shift. The moment investor sentiment shifted, these governments would default. ("Once you lose confidence, you don't get it back. You just don't.") And then what? The financial crisis of 2008 was suspended only because investors believed that governments could borrow whatever they needed to rescue their banks. What happened when the governments themselves ceased to be credible?

There was another, bigger financial crisis waiting to happen—the only question in Kyle Bass's mind was when. At the end of 2008, he thought Greece would probably be the first to go, perhaps triggering a collapse of the euro. He thought it might happen within two years, but he didn't have a lot of conviction about his timing. "Let's say it takes five years and not two," he said. "Let's say it takes seven years. Should I wait until

I see the whites of their eyes before I position myself, or should I position myself now? The answer is now. Because the moment people think it [national default] is a possibility, it's expensive. If you wait, you have to pay up for the risk."

When we met, he had just bought his first credit default swaps on the countries he and his team of analysts viewed as the most likely to be unable to pay off their debts: Greece, Ireland, Italy, Switzerland, Portugal, and Spain. He made these bets directly with the few big Wall Street firms that he felt were least likely to be allowed to fail—Goldman Sachs, J.P. Morgan, and Morgan Stanley—but, doubting their capacity to withstand a more serious crisis, he demanded that they post collateral on the trades every day. The prices he paid for default insurance, in retrospect, look absurdly cheap. Greek government default insurance cost him 11 basis points, for instance. That is, to insure $1 million of Greek government bonds against default, Hayman Capital paid a premium of $1,100 dollars a year. Bass guessed that when Greece defaulted, as it inevitably would, the country would be forced to pay down its debt by roughly 70 percent—which is to say that every $1,100 bet would return $700,000. "There's a disbelief that a developed country can default, because we have never seen it in our lifetime," said Bass. "And it's not in anyone's interest to pay attention to this. Even our own investors. They look at us and say, 'Yeah, you got subprime right. But you're always out there looking for these extremely rare events and so you think they happen more often than they do.' But I didn't go looking for this position. I was trying to understand the way the world was working, and this came to me." Now that he understood the way the world was working, he continued, he couldn't see how any sane person could do anything but prepare for another, bigger financial catastrophe. "It may not be the end of the world," he said. "But a lot of people are going to lose a lot of money. Our goal is not to be one of them."

He was totally persuasive. He was also totally incredible. A guy sitting in an office in Dallas, Texas, making sweeping claims about the future of countries he'd hardly set foot in: how on earth could he know how a bunch of people he'd never met might behave? As he laid out his ideas I had an experience I've often had, while listening to people who seem perfectly certain about uncertain events. One part of me was swept away by his argument and began to worry the world was about to collapse; the other part suspected he might be nuts. "That's great," I said, but I was already thinking about the flight I needed to catch. "But even if you're right, what can any normal person do about it?"

He stared at me as if he'd just seen an interesting sight: the world's stupidest man.

"What do you tell your mother when she asks you where to put her money?" I asked.

"Guns and gold," he said simply.

"Guns and gold," I said. So he was nuts.

"But not gold futures," he said, paying no attention to my thoughts. "You need physical gold." He explained that when the next crisis struck, the gold futures market was likely to seize up, as there were more outstanding futures contracts than available gold. People who thought they owned gold would find they owned pieces of paper instead. He opened his desk drawer, hauled out a giant gold brick, and dropped it on the desk. "We've bought a lot of this stuff."

At this point, I was giggling nervously and glancing toward the door. The future is a lot harder to predict than people on Wall Street would have you believe. A man who has been as dramatically right about the future as Kyle Bass had been about the subprime mortgage bond market collapse might easily fool himself into thinking he had a talent for being dramatically right about all sorts of other complicated things. At any rate, I was too interested in trying to figure out what had just happened in America to worry much about what was going to happen in the rest of the world, which seemed, at the time, a trivial matter. And Bass had more or less lost interest in what had just happened in America, because he thought what was about to happen all around the world was so much more important. I made my excuses, and took my leave of Dallas, and more or less dismissed him. When I wrote the book, I left Kyle Bass on the cutting-room floor.

Then the financial world began to change again—and very much as Kyle Bass had imagined it might. Entire countries started to go bust. What appeared at first to be a story chiefly about Wall Street became a story that involved every country that came into meaningful contact with Wall Street. I wrote the book about the U.S. subprime mortgage crisis and the people who had made a fortune from it, but began to travel to these other places, just to see what was up. But I traveled with a nagging question: *how did a hedge fund manager in Dallas even think to imagine these strange events?*

Two and a half years later, in the summer of 2011, I returned to Dallas to ask Kyle Bass that question. Greek credit default swaps were up from 11 basis points to 2300; Greece was just about to default on its national debt. Ireland and Portugal had required massive bailouts; and Spain and Italy had gone from being viewed as essentially riskless to nations on the brink of financial collapse. On top of it all, the Japanese Ministry of Finance was about to send a delegation to the United States to tour the big bond investment funds such as Pimco and BlackRock—to see if they could find someone, anyone, willing to buy half a trillion dollars' worth of ten-year Japanese government bonds. "This is a scenario in which no one alive has ever invested before," Bass said. "Our biggest positions now are Japan and France. If and when the dominoes fall, the worst, by far, is France. I just hope the U.S. doesn't collapse first. All my money is bet that it won't. That's my biggest fear. That I'm wrong about the chronology of events. But I'm convinced what the ultimate outcome is."

He still owned stacks of gold and platinum bars that had roughly doubled in value, but he remained on the lookout for hard stores of wealth as a hedge against what he assumed was the coming debasement of fiat currency. Nickels, for instance.

"The value of the metal in a nickel is worth six point eight cents," he said. "Did you know that?"

I didn't.

"I just bought a million dollars' worth of them," he said, and then, perhaps sensing I couldn't do the math: "twenty million nickels."

"You bought twenty million nickels?"

"Uh-huh."

"How do you buy twenty million nickels?"

"Actually, it's very difficult," he said, and then explained that he had to call his bank and talk them into ordering him twenty million nickels. The bank had finally done it, but the Federal Reserve had its own questions. "The Fed apparently called my guy at the bank," he says. "They asked him, 'Why do you want all these nickels?' So he called me and asked, 'Why do you want all these nickels?' And I said, 'I just like nickels.' "

He pulled out a photograph of his nickels and handed it to me. There they were, piled up on giant wooden pallets in a Brink's vault in downtown Dallas.

"I'm telling you, in the next two years they'll change the content of the nickel," he said. "You really ought to call your bank and buy some now."

I doubt Kyle Bass was ever the sort of person who enjoyed sitting around an office and staring at a computer screen. He enjoys the unsettled life. We hopped into his Hummer, decorated with bumper stickers (God Bless Our Troops, Especially Our Snipers) and customized to maximize the amount of fun its owner could have in it: for instance, he could press a button and, James Bond–like, coat the road behind him in giant tacks. We roared out into the Texas hill country, where, with the fortune he'd made off the subprime crisis, Kyle Bass had purchased what amounted to a fort: a forty-thousand-square-foot ranch house on thousands of acres in the middle of nowhere, with its own water supply, and an arsenal of automatic weapons and sniper rifles and small explosives to equip a battalion. That night we tore around his property in the back of his U.S. Army jeep, firing the very latest-issue U.S. Army sniper rifles, equipped with infrared scopes, at the beavers that he felt were a menace to his waterways. "There are these explosives you can buy on the Internet," he said, as we bounded over the yellow hills. "It's a molecular reaction. FedEx will deliver hundreds of pounds of these things." The few beavers that survived the initial night rifle assault would wake up to watch their dams being more or less vaporized.

"It doesn't exactly sound like a fair fight," I said.

"Beavers are rodents," he said.

Whatever else he was doing, he was clearly having fun. He'd spent two and a half years watching the global financial system, and the people who ran it, confirm his dark view of them. It didn't get him down. It thrilled him to have gotten his mind around seemingly incomprehensible events. "I'm not someone who is hell-bent on being negative his whole life," he said. "I think this is something we need to go through. It's atonement. It's atonement for the sins of the past."

Once again a hedge fund manager had been more or less right, and the world had been more or less wrong. Now seemed as good a time as any to pose the question that had nagged at me for more than two years. Here you are, I said, in so many words, an essentially provincial hedge fund manager in Dallas, Texas, whose entire adult life has been lived within a few miles of this place. You speak no foreign languages. You seldom travel abroad. You are deeply patriotic: your biggest philanthropic cause is wounded veterans. You hardly know anyone who isn't American. How did it even occur to you to start spinning theories about the financial future of these distant countries?

"It was Iceland that got me going," he said. "I've always been interested in Iceland."

"But why?"

"Did you ever play Risk as a kid?" he asked. "I loved playing Risk. And I would always put all of my armies on Iceland. Because you could attack *anybody* from there."

The belief that he could attack anyone from Iceland had led Kyle Bass to learn whatever he could about Iceland, and to pay special attention when something happened in Iceland. He found out, for instance, that Iceland was held up by geographers as an example of a country with a special talent for survival against long environmental odds. "We kept saying, 'These banks are out of business.' But the government kept saving the banks," he said. "And right in the midst of this Iceland went broke. And I thought, Wow, that's interesting. How, after a thousand years of getting things right and overcoming all these natural obstacles, did they get it so wrong?"

I had my answer. His interest had started with a board game. It was ending with another kind of board game. And Iceland was, once again, a good place to start.

# I

## WALL STREET ON THE TUNDRA

Just after October 6, 2008, when Iceland effectively went bust, I spoke to a man at the International Monetary Fund who had been flown in to Reykjavík to determine if money might responsibly be lent to such a spectacularly bankrupt nation. He'd never been to Iceland, knew nothing about the place, and said he needed a map to find it. He has spent his life dealing with famously distressed countries, usually in Africa, perpetually in one kind of financial trouble or another. Iceland was entirely new to his experience: a nation of extremely well-to-do (No. 1 in the United Nations' 2008 Human Development Index), well-educated, historically rational human beings who had organized themselves to commit one of the single greatest acts of madness in financial history. "You have to understand," he told me, "Iceland is no longer a country. It is a hedge fund."

An entire nation without immediate experience or even distant memory of high finance had gazed upon the example of Wall Street and said, "We can do that." For a brief moment it appeared that they could. In 2003, Iceland's three biggest banks had assets of only a few billion dollars, about 100 percent of the country's gross domestic product. Over the next three and a half years the banking assets grew to over $140 billion and were so much greater than Iceland's GDP that it made no sense to calculate the percentage of it they accounted for. It was, as one economist put it to me, "the most rapid expansion of a banking system in the history of mankind."

At the same time, in part because the banks were also lending Icelanders money to buy stocks and real estate, the value of Icelandic stocks and real estate went through the roof. From 2003 to 2007, while the value of the U.S. stock market was doubling, the value of the Icelandic stock market multiplied nine times. Reykjavík real estate prices tripled. In 2006 the average Icelandic family was three times as wealthy as the average Icelandic family had been in 2003, and virtually all of this new wealth was, in one way or another, tied to the new investment banking industry. "Everyone was learning Black-Scholes" (the option-pricing model), says Ragnar Arnason, a professor of fishing economics at the University of Iceland, who watched students flee the economics of fishing for the economics of money. "The schools of engineering and math were offering courses on financial engineering. We had hundreds and hundreds of people studying finance." This in a country the size of Kentucky, but with fewer citizens than greater Peoria, Illinois. Peoria, Illinois, doesn't have global financial institutions, or a university devoting itself to training many hundreds of financiers, or its own currency. And yet the world was taking Iceland seriously. (March 2006 Bloomberg News headline: ICELAND'S BILLIONAIRE TYCOON "THOR" BRAVES U.S. WITH HEDGE FUND.)

Global financial ambition turned out to have a downside. When their three brand-new global-size banks collapsed, Iceland's 300,000 citizens found that they bore some kind of responsibility for $100 billion in banking losses—which works out to roughly $330,000 for every Icelandic man, woman, and child. On top of that they had tens of billions of dollars in personal losses from their own bizarre private foreign-currency speculation, and even more from the 85 percent collapse in the Icelandic stock market. The exact dollar amount of Iceland's financial hole was essentially unknowable, as it depended upon the value of the generally stable Icelandic krona, which had also crashed and was removed from the market by the government. But it was a lot.

Iceland instantly became the only nation on earth that Americans could point to and say, "Well, at least we didn't do *that*." In the end, Icelanders amassed debts amounting to 850 percent of their GDP. (The debt-drowned United

States has reached just 350 percent.) As absurdly big and important as Wall Street became in the U.S. economy, it never grew so large that the rest of the population could not, in a pinch, bail it out. Each one of the three Icelandic banks suffered losses too large for the nation to bear; taken together they were so ridiculously out of proportion that, within weeks of the collapse, a third of the population told pollsters that they were considering emigration.

In just three or four years an entirely new way of economic life had been grafted onto the side of this stable, collectivist society, and the graft had overwhelmed the host. "It was just a group of young kids," said the man from the IMF. "In this egalitarian society, they came in, dressed in black, and started doing business."

FIVE HUNDRED MILES northwest of Scotland the Icelandair flight lands and taxis to a terminal still painted with Landsbanki logos—Landsbanki being one of Iceland's three bankrupt banks, along with Kaupthing and Glitnir. I try to think up a metaphor for the world's expanding reservoir of defunct financial corporate sponsorships—water left in the garden hose after you've switched off the pressure?—but before I can finish, the man in the seat behind me reaches for his bag in the overhead bin and knocks the crap out of me. I will soon learn that Icelandic males, like moose, rams, and other horned mammals, see these collisions as necessary in their struggle for survival. I will also learn that this particular Icelandic male is a senior official at the Iceland Stock Exchange. At this moment, however, all I know is that a middle-aged man in an expensive suit has gone out of his way to bash bodies without apology or explanation. I stew on this apparently wanton act of hostility all the way to passport control.

You can tell a lot about a country by observing how much better they treat themselves than foreigners at the point of entry. Let it be known that Icelanders make no distinction at all. Over the control booth they've hung a charming sign that reads simply, ALL CITIZENS, and what they mean by that is not "All Icelandic Citizens" but "All Citizens of Anywhere." Everyone is from somewhere, and so we all wind up in the same line, leading to the guy behind the glass. Before you can say, "Land of contradictions," he has pretended to examine your passport and waved you on through.

Next, through a dark landscape of snow-spackled black volcanic rock that may or may not be lunar, but that looks so much as you would expect the moon to look that NASA scientists used it to acclimate the astronauts before the first moon mission. An hour later we arrive at the 101 Hotel, owned by the wife of one of Iceland's most famous failed bankers. It's cryptically named (101 is the city's richest postal code) but instantly recognizable: hip Manhattan hotel. Staff dressed in black, incomprehensible art on the walls, unread books about fashion on unused coffee tables—everything to heighten the social anxiety of a rube from the sticks but the latest edition of the *New York Observer*. It's the sort of place bankers stay because they think it's where the artists stay. Bear Stearns convened a meeting of British and American hedge fund managers here, in January 2008, to figure out how much money there was to be made betting on Iceland's collapse. (A lot.) The hotel, once jammed, is now empty, with only six of its thirty-eight rooms occupied. The restaurant is empty, too, and so are the small tables and little nooks that once led the people who weren't in them to marvel at those who were. A bankrupt Holiday Inn is just depressing; a bankrupt Ian Schrager hotel is tragic.

With the financiers who once paid a lot to stay here gone for good, I'm given a big room on the top floor with a view of the old city for half-price. I curl up in silky white sheets and reach for a book about the Icelandic economy—written in 1995, before the banking craze, when the country had little to sell to the outside world but fresh fish—and read this remarkable sentence: "Icelanders are rather suspicious of the market system as a cornerstone of economic organization, especially its distributive implications."

That's when the strange noises commence.

First, the banging of a bed frame against the wall, followed by various moans and high-pitched yells. The couple in the next room has returned for the evening. Their noises grow louder but what's strange is that no matter how loud they grow, or how clearly I can hear them, the words that accompany them remain totally incomprehensible. Finding it hard to concentrate on *The Icelandic Fisheries*, I instead try to mimic the sounds coming though my wall—but when I do my tongue is doing things in my mouth that it's never done before. The sounds from the other side of the wall are roughly those made by the Stoor hobbit in *Lord of the Rings*. *Gollum . . . Gollum! . . . Mordor . . . Mordor!* Then I realize: it's just Icelandic.

Next comes a screeching from the far side of the room. I leave the bed to examine the situation. It's the heat, sounding like a teakettle left on the stove for too long, straining to control itself. Iceland's heat isn't heat as we know it, but heat drawn directly from the earth. The default temperature of the water is scalding. Every year workers engaged in street repairs shut down the cold-water intake used to temper the hot water and some poor Icelander is essentially boiled alive in his shower. So powerful is the heat being released from the earth into my room that some great grinding, wheezing engine must be employed to prevent it from cooking me.

Finally, from outside, comes an explosion.

*Boom!*

Then another.

*Boom!*

AS IT IS mid-December, the sun rises, barely, at 10:50 A.M. and sets with enthusiasm at 3:44 P.M. This is obviously better than no sun at all, but subtly worse, as it tempts you to believe you can simulate a normal life. And whatever else this place is, it isn't normal. The point is reinforced by a twenty-six-year-old Icelander I'll call Magnus Olafsson, who, just a few weeks earlier, had been earning close to a million dollars a year trading currencies for one of the banks. Tall, white-blond, and handsome, Olafsson looks exactly as you'd expect an Icelander to look—which is to say that he looks not at all like most Icelanders, who are mousy-haired and lumpy. "My mother has enough food hoarded to open a grocery store," he says, then adds that ever since the crash Reykjavík has felt tense and uneasy.

Two months earlier, in early October, as the market for Icelandic kronur dried up, he'd sneaked away from his trading desk and gone down to the teller, where he'd extracted as much foreign cash as they'd give him and stuffed it into a sack. "All over downtown that day you saw people walking around with bags," he says. "No one ever carries bags around downtown." After work he'd gone home with his sack of cash and hidden roughly 30 grand in yen, dollars, euros, and pounds sterling inside a board game.

Before October the big-name bankers were heroes; now they are abroad, or lying low. Before October Magnus thought of Iceland as essentially free of danger; now he imagines hordes of muggers en route from foreign nations to pillage his board-game safe—and thus refuses to allow me to use his real name. "You'd figure New York would hear about this and send over planeloads of muggers," he theorizes. "Most everyone has their savings at home." As he is already unsettled, I tell him about the unsettling explosions outside my hotel room. "Yes," he says with a smile, "there's been a lot of Range Rovers catching fire lately." Then he explains.

For the past few years, some large number of Icelanders engaged in the same disastrous speculation. With local interest rates at 15.5 percent and the krona rising, they decided the smart thing to do, when they wanted to buy something they couldn't afford, was to borrow not kronur but yen and Swiss francs. They paid 3 percent interest on the yen and in the bargain made a bundle on the currency trade, as the krona kept rising. "The fishing guys pretty much discovered the trade and made it huge," says

Magnus. "But they made so much money on it that the financial stuff eventually overwhelmed the fish." They made so much money on it that the trade spread from the fishing guys to their friends.

It must have seemed like a no-brainer: buy these ever more valuable houses and cars with money you are, in effect, paid to borrow. But, in October, after the krona collapsed, the yen and Swiss francs they must repay became many times more expensive. Now many Icelanders—especially young Icelanders—own $500,000 houses with $1.5 million mortgages, and $35,000 Range Rovers with $100,000 in loans against them. To the Range Rover problem there are two immediate solutions. One is to put it on a boat, ship it to Europe, and try to sell it for a currency that still has value. The other is set it on fire and collect the insurance: *Boom!*

The rocks beneath Reykjavík may be igneous, but the city feels sedimentary: on top of several thick strata of architecture that should be called Nordic Pragmatic lies a thin layer that will almost certainly one day be known as Asshole Capitalist. The hobbit-size buildings that house the Icelandic government are charming and scaled to the city. The half-built oceanfront glass towers meant to house newly rich financiers and, in the bargain, block everyone else's view of the white bluffs across the harbor are not.

· · ·

THE BEST WAY to see any city is to walk it, but everywhere I walk Icelandic men plow into me without so much as a by-your-leave. Just for fun I march up and down the main shopping drag, playing chicken, to see if any Icelandic male would rather divert his stride than bang shoulders. Nope. On party nights—Thursday, Friday, and Saturday—when half the country appears to take it as a professional obligation to drink themselves into oblivion and wander the streets until what should be sunrise, the problem is especially acute. The bars stay open until five in the morning, and the frantic energy with which the people hit them seems more like work than work. Within minutes of entering a nightclub called Boston I get walloped, first by a bearded troll who, I'm told, ran an Icelandic hedge fund. Just as I'm recovering I get plowed over by a drunken senior staffer at the Central Bank. Perhaps because he is drunk, or perhaps because we had actually met a few hours earlier, he stops to tell me, "Vee try to tell them dat our problem was not a solfency problem but a likvitity problem, but they did not agree," then stumbles off. It's exactly what Lehman Brothers and Citigroup said: if only you'd give us the money to tide us over, we'll survive this little hiccup.

A nation so tiny and homogeneous that everyone in it knows pretty much everyone else is so fundamentally different from what one thinks of when one hears the word "nation" that it almost requires a new classification. Really, it's less a nation than one big extended family. For instance, most Icelanders are by default members of the Lutheran Church. If they want to stop being Lutherans they must write to the government and quit; on the other hand, if they fill out a form, they can start their own cult and receive a subsidy. Another example: the Reykjavík phone book lists everyone by his first name, as there are only about nine surnames in Iceland, and they are derived by prefixing the father's name to "son" or "dóttir." It's hard to see how this clarifies matters, as there seem to be only about nine first names in Iceland, too. But if you wish to reveal how little you know about Iceland, you need merely refer to someone named Siggor Sigfússon as "Mr. Sigfússon," or Kristin Pétursdóttir as "Ms. Pétursdóttir." At any rate, everyone in a conversation is just meant to know whomever you're talking about, so you never hear anyone ask, "Which Siggor do you mean?"

Because Iceland is really just one big family, it's simply annoying to go around asking Icelanders if they've met Björk. Of course they've met Björk; who *hasn't* met Björk? Who, for that matter, didn't know Björk when she was two? "Yes, I know Björk," a professor of finance at the University of Iceland says in reply to my question, in a weary tone. "She can't sing, and I know her mother from childhood, and they were both crazy. That she is so well known outside of Iceland tells me more about the world than it does about Björk."

One benefit of life inside a nation masking an extended family is that nothing needs to be explained; everyone already knows everything that needs to be known. I quickly find that it is an even greater than usual waste of time to ask directions, for instance. Just as you are meant to know which Bjornjolfer is being spoken of at any particular moment, you are meant to know where you are on the map. Two grown-ups—one a banker whose office is three blocks away—cannot tell me where to find the prime minister's office. Three more grown-ups, all within three blocks of the National Gallery of Iceland, have no idea where to find the place. When I tell the sweet middle-aged woman behind the counter at the National Museum that no Icelander seems to know how to find it, she says, "No one actually knows anything about our country. Last week we had Icelandic high school students here and their teacher asked them to name an Icelandic nineteenth-century painter. None of them could. Not a single one! One said, 'Halldór Laxness?'!" (Laxness won the 1955 Nobel Prize in Literature, the greatest global honor for an Icelander until the 1980s, when two Icelandic women, in rapid succession, captured Miss World titles.)

THE WORLD IS now pocked with cities that feel as if they are perched on top of bombs. The bombs have yet to explode, but the fuses have been lit, and there's nothing anyone can do to extinguish them. Walking around Manhattan just before the collapse of Lehman Brothers, you saw empty stores, empty streets, and, even when it was raining, empty taxis; the people had fled before the bomb exploded. Reykjavík had the same feel of incipient doom, but the fuse burned strangely. The government mandates three months' severance pay, and so the many laid-off bankers were paid until early February, when the government promptly fell. Against a basket of foreign currencies the krona is worth less than a third of its boom-time value. As Iceland imports everything but heat and fish, the price of just about everything is, in mid-December, about to skyrocket. A new friend who works for the government tells me that she went into a store to buy a lamp. The clerk told her he had sold the last of the lamps she was after but offered to order it for her, from Sweden—at nearly three times the old price.

Still, a society that has been ruined overnight doesn't look much different from how it did the day before, when it believed itself to be richer than ever. The Central Bank of Iceland is a case in point. Almost certainly Iceland will adopt the euro as its currency, and the krona will cease to exist. Without it there is no need for a central bank to maintain the stability of the local currency and control interest rates. Inside the place stews David Oddsson, the architect of Iceland's rise and fall. Back in the 1980s, Oddsson had fallen under the spell of Milton Friedman, the brilliant economist who was able to persuade even those who spent their lives working for the government that government was a waste of life. So Oddsson went on a quest to give Icelandic people their freedom, by which he meant freedom from government controls of any sort. As prime minister he lowered taxes, privatized industry, freed up trade, and, finally, in 2002, privatized the banks. At length, weary of prime-ministering, he got himself appointed governor of the Central Bank—even though he had no experience in banking and was, by training, a poet.

After the collapse, this disciple of Milton Friedman holed up in his office inside the bank, declining all requests for interviews. Senior government officials tell me, seriously, that they assume he spends most of his time writing poetry. (In February 2009 he would be asked by a new government to leave.) On the outside, however, the Central Bank of Iceland is still an elegant black temple set against the snowy bluffs across the harbor. Sober-looking men still enter and exit. Small boys on sleds rocket down the slope beside it, giving not a rat's ass that they are playing at ground zero of the global calamity. It all looks the same as it did before the crash, even though it couldn't be more different. The fuse is burning its way toward the bomb.

When Neil Armstrong took his small step from *Apollo 11* and looked around, he probably thought, Wow, sort of like Iceland—even though the moon was nothing like Iceland. But then, he was a tourist, and a tourist can't help but have a distorted opinion of a place: he meets unrepresentative people, has unrepresentative experiences, and runs around imposing upon the place the fantastic mental pictures he had in his head when he got there. When Iceland became a tourist in global high finance it had the same problem as Neil Armstrong. Icelanders are among the most inbred human beings on earth—geneticists often use them for research. They inhabited their remote island for 1,100 years without so much as dabbling in leveraged buyouts (LBOs), hostile takeovers, derivatives trading, or even small-scale financial fraud. When, in 2003, they sat down at the same table with Goldman Sachs and Morgan Stanley, they had only the roughest idea of what an investment banker did and how he behaved—most of it gleaned from young Icelanders' experiences at various American business schools. And so what they did with money probably says as much about the American soul, circa 2003, as it does about Icelanders. They understood instantly, for instance, that finance had less to do with productive enterprise than trading bits of paper among themselves. And when they lent money they didn't simply facilitate enterprise but bankrolled friends and family, so that they might buy and own things, like real investment bankers: Beverly Hills condos, British soccer teams and department stores, Danish airlines and media companies, Norwegian banks, Indian power plants.

That was the biggest American financial lesson the Icelanders took to heart: the importance of buying as many assets as possible with borrowed money, as asset prices only rose. By 2007, Icelanders owned roughly fifty times more foreign assets than they had in 2002. They bought private jets and third homes, in London and Copenhagen. They paid vast sums of money for services no one in Iceland had theretofore ever imagined wanting. "A guy had a birthday party, and he flew in Elton John for a million dollars to sing two songs," the head of the Left-Green Movement, Steingrimur Sigfússon, tells me with fresh incredulity. "And apparently not very well." They bought stakes in businesses they knew nothing about and told the people running them what to do—just like real American investment bankers! For instance, an investment company called FL Group—a major shareholder in Glitnir bank—bought an 8.25 percent stake in American Airlines' parent corporation. No one inside FL Group had ever actually run an airline; no one in FL Group even had meaningful work experience at an airline. That didn't stop FL Group from telling American Airlines how to run an airline. "After taking a close look at the company over an extended period of time," FL Group CEO Hannes Smárason, a graduate of MIT's Sloan School, got himself quoted saying, in his press release, not long after he bought his shares, "our suggestions include monetizing assets . . . that can be used to reduce debt or return capital to shareholders."

Nor were the Icelanders particularly choosy about what they bought. I spoke with a hedge fund in New York that, in late 2006, spotted what it took to be an easy mark: a weak Scandinavian bank getting weaker. It established a short position, and then, out of nowhere, came Kaupthing to take a 10 percent stake in this soon to be defunct enterprise, driving up the share price to absurd levels. I spoke to another hedge fund in London so perplexed by the many bad LBOs Icelandic banks were financing that it hired private investigators to figure out what was going on in the Icelandic financial system. The investigators produced a chart detailing a byzantine web of interlinked entities that boiled down to this: a handful of guys in Iceland who had no experience in finance were taking out tens of billions of dollars in short-term loans from abroad. They were then relending this money to themselves and their friends to buy assets—the banks, soccer teams, etc. Since the entire world's assets were rising—thanks in part to people like these Icelandic lunatics paying crazy prices for them—they appeared to be making money. Yet another hedge fund manager explained Icelandic banking to me this way: you have a dog, and I have a cat. We agree that each is worth a billion dollars. You sell me the dog for a billion, and I sell you the cat for a billion. Now we are no longer pet owners but Icelandic banks, with a billion dollars in new assets. "They created fake capital by trading assets amongst themselves at inflated values," says a London hedge fund manager. "This was how the banks and investment companies grew and grew. But they were lightweights in the international markets."

ON FEBRUARY 3, Tony Shearer, the former CEO of a British merchant bank called Singer & Friedlander, offered a glimpse of the inside when he appeared before a House of Commons committee to describe his bizarre experience of being acquired by an Icelandic bank.

Singer & Friedlander had been around since 1907 and was famous for, among other things, giving George Soros his start. In November 2003, Shearer learned that Kaupthing, of whose existence he was totally unaware, had just taken a 9.5 percent stake in his bank. Normally, when a bank tries to buy another bank, it seeks to learn something about it. Shearer offered to meet with Kaupthing's chairman, Sigurdur Einarsson; Einarsson had no interest. When Kaupthing raised its stake to 19.5 percent, Shearer finally flew to Reykjavík to see who on earth these Icelanders were. "They were very different," he told the House of Commons committee. "They ran their business in a very strange way. Everyone there was incredibly young. They were all from the same community in Reykjavík. And they had no idea what they were doing."

He examined Kaupthing's annual reports and discovered some amazing facts: this giant international bank had only one board member who was not Icelandic, for instance. Its directors all had four-year contracts, and the bank had lent them £19 million to buy shares in Kaupthing, along with options to sell those shares back to the bank at a guaranteed profit. Virtually the entire bank's stated profits were caused by its marking up assets it had bought at inflated prices. "The actual amount of profits that were coming from what I'd call banking was less than 10 percent," said Shearer.

In a sane world the British regulators would

have stopped the new Icelandic financiers from devouring the ancient British merchant bank. Instead, the regulators ignored a letter Shearer wrote to them. A year later, in January 2005, he received a phone call from the British takeover panel. "They wanted to know," says Shearer, "why our share price had risen so rapidly over the past couple of days. So I laughed and said, 'I think you'll find the reason is that Mr. Einarsson, the chairman of Kaupthing, said two days ago, like an idiot, that he was going to make a bid for Singer & Friedlander.'" In August 2005, Singer & Friedlander became Kaupthing Singer & Friedlander, and Shearer quit, he says, out of fear of what might happen to his reputation if he stayed. Sure enough, in October 2008, Kaupthing Singer & Friedlander went bust.

In spite of all this, when Tony Shearer was pressed by the House of Commons to characterize the Icelanders as mere street hustlers, he refused. "They were all highly educated people," he said in a tone of amazement.

HERE IS YET another way in which Iceland echoed the American model: all sorts of people, none of them Icelandic, tried to tell them they had a problem. In early 2006, for instance, an analyst named Lars Christensen and three of his colleagues at Denmark's biggest bank, Danske Bank, wrote a report that said Iceland's financial system was growing at a mad pace and was on a collision course with disaster. "We actually wrote the report because we were worried our clients were getting too interested in Iceland," he tells me. "Iceland was the most extreme of everything." Christensen then flew to Iceland and gave a speech to reinforce his point, only to be greeted with anger. "The Icelandic banks took it personally," he says. "We were being threatened with lawsuits. I was told, 'You're Danish, and you are angry with Iceland because Iceland is doing so well.' Basically it all had to do with what happened in 1944," when Iceland declared its independence from Denmark. "The reaction wasn't, 'These guys might be right.' It was, 'No! It's a conspiracy. They have bad motives.'" The Danish were just jealous!

The Danske Bank report alerted hedge funds in London to an opportunity: shorting Iceland. They investigated and found this incredible web of cronyism: bankers buying stuff from one another at inflated prices, borrowing tens of billions of dollars and relending it to the members of their little Icelandic tribe, who then used it to buy up a messy pile of foreign assets. "Like any new kid on the block," says Theo Phanos, of Trafalgar Asset Managers, in London, "they were picked off by various people who sold them the lowest-quality assets—second-tier airlines, sub-scale retailers. They were in all the worst LBOs."

But from the prime minister on down, Iceland's leaders attacked the messenger. "The attacks . . . give off an unpleasant odor of unscrupulous dealers who have decided to make a last stab at breaking down the Icelandic financial system," said Central Bank chairman Oddsson in March 2009. The chairman of Kaupthing publicly fingered four hedge funds that he said were deliberately seeking to undermine Iceland's financial miracle. "I don't know where the Icelanders get this notion," says Paul Ruddock, of Lansdowne Partners, one of those fingered. "We only once traded in an Icelandic stock and it was a very short-term trade. We started to take legal action against the chairman of Kaupthing after he made public accusations against us that had no truth, and then he withdrew them."

One of the hidden causes of the current global financial crisis is that the people who saw it coming had more to gain from it by taking short positions than they did by trying to publicize the problem. Plus, most of the people who could credibly charge Iceland—or, for that matter, Lehman Brothers—with financial crimes could be dismissed as crass profiteers, talking their own book. Back in April 2006, however, an emeritus professor of economics at the University of Chicago named Bob Aliber took an interest in Iceland. Aliber found himself at the London Business School, listening to a talk on Iceland, about which he knew nothing. He recognized the signs instantly. Digging into the data, he found in Iceland the outlines of what was so clearly a historic act of financial madness that it belonged in a textbook. "The Perfect Bubble," Aliber calls Iceland's financial rise, and he has the textbook in the works: an updated version of Charles Kindleberger's 1978 classic, *Manias, Panics, and Crashes*. Aliber is editing the new edition. In it, Iceland, he decided back in 2006, would now have its own little box, along with the South Sea Bubble and tulip mania—even though Iceland had yet to crash. For him the actual crash was a mere formality.

Word spread in Icelandic economic circles that this distinguished professor at Chicago had taken a special interest in Iceland. In May 2008, Aliber was invited by the University of Iceland's economics department to give a speech. To an audience of students, bankers, and journalists, he explained that Iceland, far from having an innate talent for high finance, had all the markings of a giant bubble, but he spoke the technical language of academic economists. ("Monetary Turbulence and the Icelandic Economy," he called his speech.) In the following Q&A session someone asked him to predict the future, and he lapsed into plain English. As an audience member recalls, Aliber said, "I give you nine months. Your banks are dead. Your bankers are either stupid or greedy. And I'll bet they are on planes trying to sell their assets right now."

The Icelandic bankers in the audience sought to prevent newspapers from reporting the speech. Several academics suggested that Aliber deliver his alarming analysis to Iceland's Central Bank. Somehow that never happened. "The Central Bank said they were too busy to see him," says one of the professors who tried to arrange the meeting, "because they were preparing the *Report on Financial Stability*." For his part Aliber left Iceland thinking that he'd caused such a stir he might not be allowed back into the country. "I got the feeling," he told me, "that the only reason they brought me in was that they needed an outsider to say these things—that an insider wouldn't say these things, because he'd be afraid of getting into trouble." And yet he remains extremely fond of his hosts. "They are a very curious people," he says, laughing. "I guess that's the point, isn't it?"

Icelanders—or at any rate Icelandic men—had their own explanations for why, when they leapt into global finance, they broke world records: the natural superiority of Icelanders. Because they were small and isolated, it had taken 1,100 years for them—and the world—to understand and exploit their natural gifts, but now that the world was flat and money flowed freely, unfair disadvantages had vanished. Iceland's president,

Ólafur Ragnar Grimsson, gave speeches abroad in which he explained why Icelanders were banking prodigies. "Our heritage and training, our culture and home market, have provided a valuable advantage," he said, then went on to list nine of these advantages, ending with how unthreatening to others Icelanders are. ("Some people even see us as fascinating eccentrics who can do no harm.") There were many, many expressions of this same sentiment, most of them in Icelandic. "There were research projects at the university to explain why the Icelandic business model was superior," says Gylfi Zoega, chairman of the economics department. "It was all about our informal channels of communication and ability to make quick decisions and so forth."

"We were always told that the Icelandic businessmen were so clever," says university finance professor and former banker Vilhjálmur Bjarnason. "They were very quick. And when they bought something they did it very quickly. Why was that? That is usually because the seller is very satisfied with the price."

You didn't need to be Icelandic to join the cult of the Icelandic banker. German banks put $21 billion into Icelandic banks. The Netherlands gave them $305 million, and Sweden kicked in $400 million. UK investors, lured by the eye-popping 14 percent annual returns, forked over $30 billion—$28 billion from companies and individuals and the rest from pension funds, hospitals, universities, and other public institutions. Oxford University alone lost $50 million.

Maybe because there are so few Icelanders in the world, we know next to nothing about them. We assume they are more or less Scandinavian— a gentle people who just want everyone to have the same amount of everything. They are not. They have a feral streak in them, like a horse that's just pretending to be broken.

**AFTER THREE DAYS** in Reykjavík, I receive, more or less out of the blue, two phone calls. The first is from a producer of a leading current-events TV show. All of Iceland watches her show, she says, then asks if I'd come on and be interviewed.

"About what?" I ask.

"We'd like you to explain our financial crisis," she says.

"I've only been here three days!" I say.

It doesn't matter, she says, as no one in Iceland understands what's happened. They'd enjoy hearing someone try to explain it, even if that person didn't have any idea what he was talking about—which goes to show, I suppose, that not everything in Iceland is different from other places. As I demur, another call comes, from the prime minister's office.

Iceland's then prime minister, Geir Haarde, was

also the head of the Independence Party, which governed the country from 1991 to 2009. It ruled in loose coalition with the Social Democrats and the Progressive Party. (Iceland's fourth major party is the Left-Green Movement.) That a nation of 300,000 people, all of whom are related by blood, needs four major political parties suggests either a talent for disagreement or an unwillingness to listen to one another. In any case, of the four parties, the Independents express the greatest faith in free markets. The Independence Party is the party of the fishermen. It is also, as an old schoolmate of the prime minister's puts it to me, "all men, men, men. Not a woman in it."

Walking into the PM's minute headquarters, I expect to be stopped and searched, or at least asked for photo identification. Instead I find a single policeman sitting behind a reception desk, feet up on the table, reading a newspaper. He glances up, bored. "I'm here to see the prime minister," I say for the first time in my life. He's unimpressed. Anyone here can see the prime minister. Half a dozen people will tell me that one of the reasons Icelanders thought they would be taken seriously as global financiers is that all Icelanders feel important. One reason they all feel important is that they all can go see the prime minister anytime they like.

What the prime minister might say to the

Icelanders about their collapse is an open question. There's a charming lack of financial experience in Icelandic financial-policymaking circles. The minister for business affairs is a philosopher. The finance minister is a veterinarian. The Central Bank governor is a poet. Haarde, though, is a trained economist—just not a very good one. The economics department at the University of Iceland has him pegged as a B-minus student. As a group, the Independence Party's leaders have a reputation for not knowing much about finance and for refusing to avail themselves of experts who do. An Icelandic professor at the London School of Economics named Jon Danielsson, who specializes in financial panics, has had his offer to help spurned; so have several well-known financial economists at the University of Iceland. Even the advice of really smart Central Bankers from seriously big countries went ignored. It's not hard to see why the Independence Party and its prime minister fail to appeal to Icelandic women: they are the guy driving his family around in search of some familiar landmark and refusing, over his wife's complaints, to stop and ask directions.

"Why are you interested in Iceland?" he asks, as he strides into the room with the force and authority of the leader of a much larger nation. And it's a good question.

As it turns out, he's not actually stupid, but political leaders seldom are, no matter how much the people who elected them insist that it must be so. He does indeed say things that could not possibly be true, but they are only the sorts of fibs that prime ministers are hired to tell. He claims that the krona is once again an essentially stable currency, for instance, when the truth is it doesn't trade in international markets. The krona is simply assigned an arbitrary value by the government for select purposes. Icelanders abroad have already figured out not to use their Visa cards, for fear of being charged the real exchange rate, whatever that might be.

The prime minister would like me to believe that he saw Iceland's financial crisis taking shape but could do little about it. ("We could not say publicly our fears about the banks, because you create the very thing you are seeking to avoid: a panic.") By implication it was not politicians like him but financiers who were to blame. On some level the people agree: the guy who ran the Baugur investment group had snowballs chucked at him as he dashed from the 101 Hotel to his limo; the guy who ran Kaupthing Bank turned up at the National Theatre and, as he took his seat, was booed. But, for the most part, the big shots have fled Iceland for London, or are lying low, leaving the poor prime minister to shoulder the blame and face the angry demonstrators, led by folksinging activist Hördur Torfason, who assemble every weekend outside Parliament.

Haarde has his story, and he's sticking to it: foreigners entrusted their capital to Iceland, and Iceland put it to good use, but then, on September 15, 2008, Lehman Brothers failed and foreigners panicked and demanded their capital back. Iceland was ruined not by its own recklessness but by a global tsunami. The problem with this story is that it fails to explain why the tsunami struck Iceland, as opposed to, say, Tonga.

But I didn't come to Iceland to argue. I came to understand. "There's something I really want to ask you," I say.

"Yes?"

"Is it true that you've been telling people that it's time to stop banking and go fishing?"

A great line, I thought. Succinct, true, and to the point. But I'd heard about it thirdhand, from a New York hedge fund manager. The prime minister fixes me with a self-consciously stern gaze. "That's a gross exaggeration," he says.

"I thought it made sense," I say uneasily.

"I never said that!"

Obviously, I've hit some kind of nerve, but which kind I cannot tell. Is he worried that to have said such a thing would make him seem a fool? Or does he still think that fishing, as a profession, is somehow less dignified than banking?

• • •

AT LENGTH, I return to the hotel to find, for the first time in four nights, no empty champagne bottles outside my neighbors' door. The Icelandic couple whom I had envisioned as being on one last blowout have packed and gone home. For four nights I have endured their orc shrieks from the other side of the hotel wall; now all is silent. It's possible to curl up in bed with "The Economic Theory of a Common-Property Resource: The Fishery." One way or another, the wealth in Iceland comes from the fish, and if you want to understand what Icelanders did with their money you had better understand how they came into it in the first place.

The brilliant paper was written back in 1954 by H. Scott Gordon, an Indiana University economist. It describes the plight of the fisherman—and seeks to explain "why fishermen are not wealthy, despite the fact that fishery resources of the sea are the richest and most indestructible available to man." The problem is that, because the fish are everybody's property, they are nobody's property. Anyone can catch as many fish as he likes, so people fish right up to the point where fishing becomes unprofitable—for everybody. "There is in the spirit of every fisherman the hope of the 'lucky catch,'" wrote Gordon. "As those who know fishermen well have often testified, they are gamblers and incurably optimistic."

Fishermen, in other words, are a lot like American investment bankers. Their over-confidence leads them to impoverish not just themselves but also their fishing grounds. Simply limiting the number of fish caught won't solve the problem; it will just heighten the competition for the fish and drive down profits. The goal isn't to get fishermen to overspend on more nets or bigger boats. The goal is to catch the maximum number of fish with minimum effort. To attain it, you need government intervention.

This insight is what led Iceland to go from being one of the poorest countries in Europe circa 1900 to being one of the richest circa 2000. Iceland's big change began in the early 1970s, after a couple of years when the fish catch was terrible. The best fishermen returned for a second year in a row without their usual haul of cod and haddock, so the Icelandic government took radical action: they privatized the fish. Each fisherman was assigned a quota, based roughly on his historical catches. If you were a big-time Icelandic fisherman you got this piece of paper that entitled you to, say, 1 percent of the total catch allowed to be pulled from Iceland's waters that season. Before each season the scientists at the Marine Research Institute would determine the total number of cod or haddock that could be caught without damaging the long-term health of the fish population; from year to year, the numbers of fish you could catch changed. But your percentage of the annual haul was fixed, and this piece of paper entitled you to it in perpetuity.

Even better, if you didn't want to fish you could sell your quota to someone who did. The quotas thus drifted into the hands of the people to whom they were of the greatest value, the best fishermen, who could extract the fish from the sea with maximum efficiency. You could also take your quota to the bank and borrow against it, and the bank had no trouble assigning a dollar value to your share of the cod pulled, without competition, from the richest cod-fishing grounds on earth. The fish had not only been privatized, they had been securitized.

IT WAS HORRIBLY unfair: a public resource—all the fish in the Icelandic sea—was simply turned over to a handful of lucky Icelanders. Overnight, Iceland had its first billionaires, and they were all fishermen. But as social policy it was ingenious: in a single stroke the fish became a source of real, sustainable wealth rather than shaky sustenance. Fewer people were spending less effort catching more or less precisely the right number of fish to maximize the long-term value of Iceland's fishing grounds. The new wealth transformed Iceland— and turned it from the backwater it had been for 1,100 years to the place that spawned Björk. If Iceland has become famous for its musicians it's because Icelanders now have time to play music, and much else. Iceland's youth are paid to study abroad, for instance, and encouraged to cultivate themselves in all sorts of interesting ways. Since its fishing policy transformed Iceland, the place has become, in effect, a machine for turning cod into PhDs.

But this, of course, creates a new problem: people with PhDs don't want to fish for a living. They need something else to do.

And that something is probably not working in the industry that exploits Iceland's other main natural resource: energy. The waterfalls and boiling lava generate vast amounts of cheap power, but, unlike oil, it cannot be profitably exported. Iceland's power is trapped in Iceland, and if there is something poetic about the idea of trapped power, there is also something prosaic in how the Icelanders have come to terms with the problem. They asked themselves: What can we do that other people will pay money for that requires huge amounts of power? The answer was: smelt aluminum.

Notice that no one asked, What might Icelanders want to do? Or even: What might Icelanders be especially suited to do? No one thought that Icelanders might have some natural gift for smelting aluminum, and, if anything, the opposite proved true. Alcoa, the biggest aluminum company in the country, encountered two problems peculiar to Iceland when, in 2004, it set about erecting its giant smelting plant. The first was the so-called hidden people—or, to put it more plainly, elves—in whom some large number of Icelanders, steeped long and thoroughly in their rich folkloric culture, sincerely believe. Before Alcoa could build its smelter it had to defer to a government expert to scour the enclosed plant site and certify that no elves were on or under it. It was a delicate corporate situation, an Alcoa spokesman told me, because they had to pay hard cash to declare the site elf-free, but, as he put it, "we couldn't as a company be in a position of acknowledging the existence of hidden people." The other, more serious problem was the Icelandic male: he took more safety risks than aluminum workers in other nations did. "In manufacturing," says the Alcoa spokesman, "you want people who follow the rules and fall in line. You don't want them to be heroes. You don't want them to try to fix something it's not their job to fix, because they might blow up the place." The Icelandic male had a propensity to try to fix something it wasn't his job to fix.

Back away from the Icelandic economy and you can't help but notice something really strange about it: the people have cultivated themselves to the point where they are unsuited for the work available to them. All these exquisitely schooled, sophisticated people, each and every one of whom feels special, are presented with two mainly horrible ways to earn a living: trawler fishing and aluminum smelting. There are, of course, a few jobs in Iceland that any refined, educated person might like to do. Certifying the nonexistence of elves, for instance. ("This will take at least six months—it can be very tricky.") But not nearly so many as the place needs, given its talent for turning cod into PhDs. At the dawn of the twenty-first century, Icelanders were still waiting for some task more suited to their filigreed minds to turn up inside their economy so they might do it.

Enter investment banking.

FOR THE FIFTH time in as many days I note a slight tension at any table where Icelandic men and Icelandic women are both present. The male exhibits the global male tendency not to talk to the females—or, rather, not to include them in the conversation—unless there is some obvious sexual motive. But that's not the problem, exactly. Watching Icelandic men and women together is like watching toddlers. They don't play together but in parallel; they overlap even less organically than men and women in other developed countries, which is really saying something. It isn't that the women are oppressed, exactly. On paper, by historical global standards, they have it about as good as women anywhere: good public health care, high participation in the workforce, equal rights. What Icelandic women appear to lack—at least to a tourist who has watched them for all of ten days—is a genuine connection to Icelandic men. The Independence Party is mostly male; the Social Democrats, mostly female. (On February 1, 2009, when the reviled Geir Haarde finally stepped aside, he was replaced by Johanna Sigurdardottir, a Social Democrat, and Iceland got not just a female prime minister but the modern world's first openly gay head of state—she is married to another woman.) Everyone knows everyone else, but when I ask Icelanders for leads, the men always refer me to other men, and the women to other women. It was a man, for instance, who suggested I speak to Stefan Alfsson.

**LEAN AND HUNGRY-LOOKING,** wearing genuine rather than designer stubble, Alfsson still looks more like a trawler captain than a financier. He went to sea at sixteen and, in the off-season, to school to study fishing. He was made captain of an Icelandic fishing trawler at the shockingly young age of twenty-three and was regarded, I learned from other men, as something of a fishing prodigy—which is to say he had a gift for catching his quota of cod and haddock in the least amount of time. And yet, in January 2005, at thirty, he up and quit fishing to join the currency-trading department of Landsbanki. He speculated in the financial markets for nearly two years, until the great bloodbath of October 2008, when he was sacked, along with every other Icelander who called himself a "trader." His job, he says, was to sell people, mainly his fellow fishermen, on what he took to be a can't-miss speculation: borrow yen at 3 percent, use them to buy Icelandic kronur, and then invest those kronur at 16 percent. "I think it is easier to take someone in the fishing industry and teach him about currency trading," he says, "than to take someone from the banking industry and teach them how to fish."

He then explained why fishing wasn't as simple as I thought. It's risky, for a start, especially as practiced by the Icelandic male. "You don't want to have some sissy boys on your crew," he says, especially as Icelandic captains are famously manic in their fishing styles. "I had a crew of Russians once," he says, "and it wasn't that they were lazy, but the Russians are always at the same pace." When a storm struck, the Russians would stop fishing, because it was too dangerous. "The Icelanders would fish in all conditions," says Stefan, "fish until it is impossible to fish. They like to take the risks. If you go overboard, the probabilities are not in your favor. I'm thirty-three, and I already have two friends who have died at sea."

It took years of training for him to become a captain, and even then it happened only by a stroke of luck. When he was twenty-three and a first mate, the captain of his fishing boat quit. The boat owner went looking for a replacement and found an older fellow, retired, who was something of an Icelandic fishing legend, the wonderfully named Snorri Snorrasson. "I took two trips with this guy," Stefan says. "I have never in my life slept so little, because I was so eager to learn. I slept two or three hours a night because I was sitting beside him, talking to him. I gave him all the respect in the world—it's difficult to describe all he taught me. The reach of the trawler. The most efficient angle of the net. How do you act on the sea. If you have a bad day, what do you do? If you're fishing at this depth, what do you do? If it's not working, do you move in depth or space? In the end it's just so much feel. In this time I learned infinitely more than I learned in school. Because how do you learn to fish in school?"

This marvelous training was as fresh in his mind as if he'd received it yesterday, and the thought of it makes his eyes mist.

"You spent *seven* years learning every little nuance of the fishing trade before you were granted the gift of learning from this great captain?" I ask.

"Yes."

"And even then you had to sit at the feet of this great master for many months before you felt as if you knew what you were doing?"

"Yes."

"Then why did you think you could become a banker and speculate in financial markets without a day of training?"

"That's a very good question," he says. He thinks for a minute. "For the first time this evening I lack a word." As I often think I know exactly what I am doing even when I don't, I find myself sympathetic.

"What, exactly, was your job?" I ask, to let him off the hook, catch and release being the current humane policy in Iceland.

"I started as a . . ."—now he begins to laugh—"an adviser to companies on currency risk hedging. But given my aggressive nature I went more and more into plain speculative trading." Many of his clients were other fishermen, and fishing companies, and they, like him, had learned that if you don't take risks you don't catch the fish. "The clients were only interested in 'hedging' if it meant making money," he says, and begins to laugh hysterically.

"Did you even *like* banking?" I ask.

"I never had any respect for bankers," he says, still gasping for breath. "To this day one of my favorite phrases is: *never trust a banker.*"

IN RETROSPECT, THERE are some obvious questions an Icelander living through the past five years might have asked himself. For example: Why should Iceland suddenly be so seemingly essential to global finance? Or: Why do giant countries that invented modern banking suddenly need Icelandic banks to stand between their depositors and their borrowers—to decide who gets capital and who does not? And: If Icelanders have this incredible natural gift for finance, how did they keep it so well hidden for 1,100 years? At the very least, in a place where everyone knows everyone else or his sister, you might have thought that the moment Stefan Alfsson walked into Landsbanki ten people would have said, "Stefan, you're a fisherman!" But they didn't. To a shocking degree, they still don't. "If I went back to banking," says the Icelandic cod fisherman, now wearing an entirely straight face, "I would be a private-banking guy."

BACK IN 2001, as the Internet boom turned into a bust, MIT's *Quarterly Journal of Economics* published an intriguing paper called "Boys Will Be Boys: Gender, Overconfidence, and Common Stock Investment." The authors, Brad Barber and Terrance Odean, gained access to the trading activity in over 35,000 households, and used it to compare the habits of men and women. What they found, in a nutshell, is that men not only trade more often than women but do so from a false faith in their own financial judgment. Single men traded less sensibly than married men, and married men traded less sensibly than single women: the less the female presence, the less rational the approach to trading in the markets.

One of the distinctive traits about Iceland's disaster, and Wall Street's, is how little women had to do with it. Women worked in the banks, but not in the risk-taking jobs. As far as I can tell, during Iceland's boom, there was just one woman in a senior position inside an Icelandic bank. Her name is Kristin Pétursdóttir, and by 2005 she had risen to become deputy CEO for Kaupthing in London. "The financial culture is very male-dominated," she says. "The culture is quite extreme. It is a pool of sharks. Women just despise the culture." Pétursdóttir still enjoyed finance. She just didn't like the way Icelandic men did it, and so, in 2006, she quit her job. "People said I was crazy," she says, but she wanted to create a financial services business run entirely by women. To bring, as she puts it, "more feminine values to the world of finance."

Today her firm is, among other things, one of the very few profitable financial businesses left in Iceland. After the stock exchange collapsed, the money flooded in. A few days before we met, for instance, she heard banging on the front door early one morning and opened it to discover a little old man. "I'm so fed up with this whole system," he said. "I just want some women to take care of my money."

It was with that in mind that I walked, on my last afternoon in Iceland, into the Saga Museum. Its goal is to glorify the Sagas, the great twelfth- and thirteenth-century Icelandic prose epics, but the effect of its life-size dioramas is more like that of modern reality TV. Not statues carved from silicone but actual ancient Icelanders, or actors posing as ancient Icelanders, as shrieks and bloodcurdling screams issue from the PA system: a Catholic bishop named Jón Arason having his head chopped off; a heretic named Sister Katrin being burned at the stake; a battle scene in which a blood-drenched Viking plunges his sword toward the heart of a prone enemy. The goal was verisimilitude, and to achieve it no expense was spared. Passing one tableau of blood and guts and moving on to the next, I caught myself glancing over my shoulder to make sure some Viking wasn't following me with a battle-ax. The effect was so disorienting that when I reached the end and found a Japanese woman immobile and reading on a bench, I had to poke her on the shoulder to make sure she was real.

This is the past Icelanders supposedly cherish: a history of conflict and heroism. Of seeing who is willing to bump into whom with the most force. There may be plenty of women in it, but it is chiefly a history of men.

When you borrow a lot of money to create a false prosperity, you import the future into the present. It isn't the actual future so much as some grotesque silicone version of it. Leverage buys you a glimpse of a prosperity you haven't really earned. The striking thing about the future the Icelandic male briefly imported was how much it resembled the past that he celebrates. I'm betting now they've seen their false future the Icelandic female will have a great deal more to say about the actual one.

# II

## AND THEY
## INVENTED MATH

After an hour on a plane, two in a taxi, three on a decrepit ferry, and then four more on buses driven madly along the tops of sheer cliffs by Greeks on cell phones, I rolled up to the front door of the vast and remote monastery. The spit of land poking into the Aegean Sea felt like the end of the earth, and just as silent. It was late afternoon, and the monks were either praying or napping, but one remained on duty at the guard booth to greet visitors. He guided me along with seven Greek pilgrims to an ancient dormitory, beautifully restored, where two more solicitous monks offered ouzo, pastries, and keys to cells. I sensed something missing, and then realized: no one had asked for a credit card. The monastery was not merely efficient but free. One of the monks then said the next event would be the church service: Vespers. The next event, it will emerge, will almost always be a church service. There were thirty-seven different chapels inside the monastery's walls; finding the service is going to be like finding Waldo, I thought.

"Which church?" I asked the monk.

"Just follow the monks after they rise," he said. Then he looked me up and down more closely. He wore an impossibly long and wild black beard, long black robes, a monk's cap, and prayer beads. I wore white running shoes, light khakis, and a mauve Brooks Brothers shirt and carried a plastic laundry bag that said EAGLES PALACE HOTEL in giant letters on the side. "Why have you come?" he asked.

That was a good question. Not for church; I was there for money. The tsunami of cheap credit that rolled across the planet between 2002 and 2007 has just now created a new opportunity for travel: financial-disaster tourism. The credit wasn't just money, it was temptation. It offered entire societies the chance to reveal aspects of their characters they could not normally afford to indulge. Entire countries were told, "The lights are out, you can do whatever you want to do and no one will ever know." What they wanted to do with money in the dark varied. Americans wanted to own homes far larger than they could afford, and to allow the strong to exploit the weak. Icelanders wanted to stop fishing and become investment bankers, and to allow their alpha males to reveal a theretofore suppressed megalomania. The Germans wanted to be even more German; the Irish wanted to stop being Irish. All these different societies were touched by the same event, but each responded to it in its own peculiar way. No response was as peculiar as the Greeks', however: anyone who had spent even a few days talking to people in charge of the place could see that. But to see just how peculiar it was, you had to come to this monastery.

I had my reasons for being here. But I was pretty sure that if I told the monk what they were, he'd throw me out. And so I lied. "They say this is the holiest place on earth," I said.

I'd arrived in Athens just a few days earlier, exactly one week before the next planned riot, and a few days after German politicians suggested that the Greek government, to pay off its debts, should sell its islands and perhaps throw some ancient ruins into the bargain. Greece's new socialist prime minister, George Papandreou, had felt compelled to deny that he was actually thinking of selling any islands. Moody's, the rating agency, had just lowered Greece's credit rating to the level that turned all Greek government bonds into junk—and so no longer eligible to be owned by many of the investors who owned them. The resulting dumping of Greek bonds onto the market was, in the short term, no big deal, because the International Monetary Fund and the European Central Bank had between them agreed to lend Greece—a nation of about eleven million people, or two million fewer than Greater Los Angeles—up to $145 billion. In the short term Greece had been removed from the free financial markets and become a ward of other states.

That was the good news. The long-term picture was far bleaker. In addition to its roughly $400 billion (and growing) of outstanding government debt, the Greek number crunchers had just figured out that their government owed another $800 billion or more in pensions. Add it all up and you got about $1.2 trillion, or more than a quarter-million dollars for every working Greek. Against $1.2 trillion in debts, a $145 billion bailout was clearly more of a gesture than a solution. And those were just the official numbers; the truth is surely worse. "Our people went in and couldn't believe what they found," a senior IMF official told me, not long after he'd returned from the IMF's first Greek mission. "The way they were keeping track of their finances—they knew how much they had agreed to spend, but no one was keeping track of what he had actually spent. It wasn't even what you would call an emerging economy. It was a third world country."

As it turned out, what the Greeks wanted to do, once the lights went out and they were alone in the dark with a pile of borrowed money, was turn their government into a piñata stuffed with fantastic sums and give as many citizens as possible a whack at it. In just the past twelve years the wage bill of the Greek public sector has doubled, in real terms—and that number doesn't take into account the bribes collected by public officials. The average government job pays almost three times the average private-sector job. The national railroad has annual revenues of 100 million euros against an annual wage bill of 400 million, plus 300 million euros in other expenses. The average state railroad employee earns 65,000 euros a year. Twenty years ago a successful businessman turned minister of finance named Stefanos Manos pointed out that it would be cheaper to put all Greece's rail passengers into taxicabs: it's still true. "We have a railroad company which is bankrupt beyond compre-hension," Manos put it to me. "And yet there isn't a single private company in Greece with that kind of average pay." The Greek public-school system is the site of breathtaking inefficiency: one of the lowest-ranked systems in Europe, it nonetheless employs four times as many teachers per pupil as the highest-ranked, Finland's. Greeks who send their children to public schools simply assume that they will need to hire private tutors to make sure they actually learn something. There are three government-owned defense companies: together they have billions of euros in debts, and mounting losses. The retirement age for Greek jobs classified as "arduous" is as early as fifty-five for men and fifty for women. As this is also the moment when the state begins to shovel out generous pensions, more than six hundred Greek professions somehow managed to get themselves classified as arduous: hairdressers, radio announcers, waiters, musicians, and on and on and on. The Greek public health-care system spends far more on supplies than the European average—and it is not uncommon, several Greeks tell me, to see nurses and doctors leaving the job with their arms filled with paper towels and diapers and whatever else they can plunder from the supply closets.

Where waste ends and theft begins almost doesn't matter; the one masks and thus enables the other. It's simply assumed, for instance, that anyone who is working for the government is meant to be bribed. People who go to public health clinics assume they will need to bribe doctors to actually take care of them. Government ministers who have spent their lives in public service emerge from office able to afford multi-million-dollar mansions and two or three country homes.

Oddly enough, the financiers in Greece remain more or less beyond reproach. They never ceased to be anything but sleepy old commercial bankers. Virtually alone among Europe's bankers, they did not buy U.S. subprime-backed bonds, or leverage themselves to the hilt, or pay themselves huge sums of money. The biggest problem the banks had was that they had lent roughly 30 billion euros to the Greek government—where it was stolen or squandered. In Greece the banks didn't sink the country. The country sank the banks.

**THE MORNING AFTER** I landed I walked over to see the Greek minister of finance, George Papaconstantinou, whose job it is to sort out this fantastic mess. Athens somehow manages to be bright white and grubby at the same time. The most beautiful freshly painted neoclassical homes are defaced with new graffiti. Ancient ruins are everywhere, of course, but seem to have little to do with anything else. It's Los Angeles with a past.

At the dark and narrow entrance to the Ministry of Finance a small crowd of security guards screen you as you enter—then don't bother to check and see why you set off the metal detector. In the minister's antechamber six women, all on their feet, arrange his schedule. They seem frantic and harried and overworked . . . and yet he still runs late. The place generally seems as if even its better days weren't so great. The furniture is worn, the floor linoleum. The most striking thing about it is how many people it employs. Minister Papaconstantinou ("It's okay to just call me George") attended NYU and the London School of Economics in the 1980s, then spent ten years working in Paris for the OECD (Organisation for

Economic Co-operation and Development). He's open, friendly, fresh-faced, and clean-shaven, and like many people at the top of the new Greek government, he comes across less as Greek than as Anglo—indeed, almost American.

When Papaconstantinou arrived here, in October 2009, the Greek government had estimated its 2009 budget deficit at 3.7 percent. Two weeks later that number was revised upward, to 12.5 percent, and actually turned out to be nearly 14 percent. He was the man whose job it had been to figure out and explain to the world why. "The second day on the job I had to call a meeting to look at the budget," he says. "I gathered everyone from the general accounting office, and we started, like, this discovery process." Each day they discovered some incredible omission. A pension debt of a billion dollars *every year* somehow remained off the government's books, where everyone pretended it did not exist, even though the government paid it; the hole in the pension plan for the self-employed was not the 300 million euros they had assumed but 1.1 billion euros; and so on. "At the end of each day I would say, 'Okay, guys, is this all?' And they would say, 'Yeah.' The next morning there would be this little hand rising in the back of the room: 'Actually, Minister, there's this other one-hundred-to-two-hundred-million-euro gap.'"

This went on for a week. Among other things

turned up were a great number of off-the-books phony job-creation programs. "The Ministry of Agriculture had created an off-the-books unit employing 270 people to digitize the photographs of Greek public lands," the finance minister tells me. "The trouble was that none of the 270 people had any experience with digital photography. The actual professions of these people were, like, hairdressers."

By the final day of discovery, after the last little hand had gone up in the back of the room, a projected deficit of roughly 7 billion euros was actually more than 30 billion. The natural question—How is this possible?—is easily answered: until that moment, no one had bothered to count it all up. "We had no Congressional Budget Office," explains the finance minister. "There was no independent statistical service." The party in power simply gins up whatever numbers it likes, for its own purposes.

Once the finance minister had the number, he went off to his regularly scheduled monthly meetings with ministers of finance from all the European countries. As the new guy, he was given the floor. "When I told them the number, there were gasps," he said. "How could this happen? I was like, *You guys should have picked up that the number wasn't right.* But the problem was I sat behind a sign that said GREECE, not a sign that said THE NEW GREEK GOVERNMENT."

After the meeting the Dutch guy came up to him and said, "George, we know it's not your fault, but shouldn't someone go to jail?"

As he finishes his story the finance minister stresses that this isn't a simple matter of the government lying about its expenditures. "This wasn't all due to misreporting," he says. "In 2009, tax collection disintegrated, because it was an election year."

"What?"

He smiles.

"The first thing a government does in an election year is to pull the tax collectors off the streets."

"You're kidding."

Now he's laughing at me. I'm clearly naïve.

THE COSTS OF running the Greek government are only half the failed equation: there's also the matter of government revenues. The editor of one of Greece's big newspapers had mentioned to me in passing that his reporters had cultivated sources inside the country's revenue service. They'd done this not so much to expose tax fraud—which was so common in Greece that it wasn't worth writing about—but to find drug lords, human smugglers, and other, darker sorts. A handful of the tax collectors, however, were outraged by the systematic corruption of their business; it further emerged that two of them were willing to meet with me. The problem was that, for reasons neither wished to discuss, they couldn't stand the sight of each other. This, I'd be told many times by other Greeks, was very Greek.

The evening after I met with the minister of finance, I had coffee with one tax collector at one hotel, then walked down the street and had a beer with another tax collector at another hotel. Both had already suffered demotions, after their attempts to blow the whistle on colleagues who had accepted big bribes to sign off on fraudulent tax returns. Both had been removed from high-status fieldwork to low-status work in the back office, where they could no longer witness tax crimes. Each was a tiny bit uncomfortable; neither wanted anyone to know he had talked to me, as they feared losing their jobs in the tax agency. And so let's call them Tax Collector No. 1 and Tax Collector No. 2.

Tax Collector No. 1—early sixties, business suit, tightly wound but not obviously nervous—arrived with a notebook filled with ideas for fixing the Greek tax-collection agency. He just took it for granted that I knew that the only Greeks who paid their taxes were the ones who could not avoid doing so—the salaried employees of corporations, who had their taxes withheld from their paychecks. The vast economy of self-employed workers—everyone from doctors to the

79

guys who ran the kiosks that sold the *International Herald Tribune*—cheated (one big reason why Greece has the highest percentage of self-employed workers of any European country). "It's become a cultural trait," he said. "The Greek people never learned to pay their taxes. And they never did because no one is punished. No one *has ever been* punished. It's a cavalier offense—like a gentleman not opening a door for a lady."

The scale of Greek tax cheating was at least as incredible as its scope: an estimated two-thirds of Greek doctors reported incomes under 12,000 euros a year—which meant, because incomes below that amount weren't taxable, that even plastic surgeons making millions a year paid no tax at all. The problem wasn't the law—there was a law on the books that made it a jailable offense to cheat the government out of more than 150,000 euros—but its enforcement. "If the law was enforced," the tax collector said, "every doctor in Greece would be in jail." I laughed, and he gave me a stare. "I am completely serious." One reason no one is ever prosecuted—apart from the fact that prosecution would seem arbitrary, as everyone is doing it—is that the Greek courts take up to fifteen years to resolve tax cases. "The one who does not want to pay, and who gets caught, just goes to court," he says. Somewhere between 30 and 40 percent of the activity in the Greek economy that might be subject to income tax goes officially unrecorded, he says, compared with an average of about 18 percent in the rest of Europe.

The easiest way to cheat on one's taxes was to insist on being paid in cash, and fail to provide a receipt for services. The easiest way to launder cash was to buy real estate. Conveniently for the black market—and alone among European countries—Greece has no working national land registry. "You have to know where the guy bought the land—the address—to trace it back to him," says the collector. "And even then it's all handwritten and hard to decipher." But, I say, if some plastic surgeon takes a million in cash, buys a plot on a Greek island, and builds himself a villa, there would be other records—say, building permits. "The people who give the building permits don't inform the Treasury," says the tax collector. In the apparently not-so-rare cases where the tax cheat gets caught, he can simply bribe the tax collector and be done with it. There are, of course, laws against tax collectors accepting bribes, explained the collector, "but if you get caught, it can take seven or eight years to get prosecuted. So in practice no one bothers."

The systematic lying about one's income had led the Greek government to rely increasingly on taxes harder to evade: real estate and sales taxes. Real estate is taxed by formula—to take the tax collectors out of the equation—which generates a so-called objective value for each home. The boom in the Greek economy over the last decade caused the actual prices at which property changed hands to far outstrip the computer-driven appraisals. Given higher actual sales prices, the formula is meant to ratchet upward. The typical Greek citizen responded to the problem by not reporting the price at which the sale took place but instead reporting a phony price—which usually happened to be the same low number at which the dated formula had appraised it. If the buyer took out a loan to buy the house, he took out a loan for the objective value and paid the difference in cash, or with a black-market loan. As a result the "objective values" grotesquely understate the actual land values. Astonishingly, it's widely believed that all three hundred members of the Greek parliament declare the real value of their houses to be the computer-generated objective value. Or, as both the tax collector and a local real estate agent put it to me, "every single member of the Greek parliament is lying to evade taxes."

On he went, describing a system that was, in its way, a thing of beauty. It mimicked the tax-collecting systems of an advanced economy—and employed a huge number of tax collectors—while it was in fact rigged to enable an entire society to cheat on their taxes. As he rose to leave, he pointed out that the waitress at the swanky tourist hotel failed to provide us with a receipt for our coffees. "There's a reason for that," he said. "Even this hotel doesn't pay the sales tax it owes."

I walked down the street and found waiting for me, in the bar of another swanky tourist hotel, the second tax collector. Tax Collector No. 2—casual in manner and dress, beer-drinking, but terrified that others might discover he had spoken to me— also arrived with a binder full of papers, only his was stuffed with real-world examples not of Greek people but Greek companies that had cheated on their taxes. He then started to rattle off examples ("only the ones I personally witnessed"). The first was an Athenian construction company that had built seven giant apartment buildings and sold off nearly a thousand condominiums in the heart of the city. Its corporate tax bill honestly computed came to 15 million euros, but the company had paid nothing at all. Zero. To evade taxes it had done several things. First, it never declared itself a corporation; second, it employed one of the dozens of companies that do nothing but create fraudulent receipts for expenses never incurred and then, when the tax collector stumbled upon the situation, offered him a bribe. The tax collector blew the whistle and referred the case to his bosses—whereupon he found himself being tailed by a private investigator, and his phones tapped. In the end the case was resolved, with the construction company paying 2,000 euros. "After that I was taken off all tax investigations," said the tax collector, "because I was good at it."

He returned to his thick binder full of cases. He turned the page. Every page in his binder held a story similar to the one he had just told me, and he intended to tell me all of them. That's when I stopped him. I realized that if I let him go on we'd be there all night. The extent of the cheating—the amount of energy that went into it—was breathtaking. In Athens, I several times had a feeling new to me as a journalist: a complete lack of interest in what was obviously shocking material. I'd sit down with someone who knew the inner workings of the Greek government: a big-time banker, a tax collector, a deputy finance minister, a former MP. I'd take out my notepad and start writing down the stories that spilled out of them. Scandal after scandal poured forth. Twenty minutes into it I'd lose interest. There were simply too many: they could fill libraries, never mind a book.

The Greek state was not just corrupt but also corrupting. Once you saw how it worked you could understand a phenomenon that otherwise made no sense at all: the difficulty Greek people have saying a kind word about one another. Individual Greeks are delightful: funny, warm, smart, and good company. I left two dozen interviews saying to myself, "What great people!" They do not share the sentiment about one another: the hardest thing to do in Greece is to get one Greek to compliment another behind his back. No success of any kind is regarded without suspicion. Everyone is pretty sure everyone is cheating on his taxes, or bribing politicians, or taking bribes, or lying about the value of his real estate. And this total absence of faith in one another is self-reinforcing. The epidemic of lying and cheating and stealing makes any sort of civic life impossible; the collapse of civic life only encourages more lying, cheating, and stealing. Lacking faith in one another, they fall back on themselves and their families.

The structure of the Greek economy is collectivist, but the country, in spirit, is the opposite of a collective. Its real structure is every man for himself. Into this system investors had poured hundreds of billions of dollars. And the credit boom had pushed the country over the edge, into total moral collapse.

KNOWING NOTHING ELSE about the Vatopaidi monastery except that, in a perfectly corrupt society, it had somehow been identified as the soul of corruption, I made my way up to the north of Greece, in search of a bunch of monks who had found new, improved ways to work the Greek economy. The first stage was fairly easy: the plane to Greece's second city of Thessaloníki, the car being driven along narrow roads at nerve-racking speeds, and a night with a lot of Bulgarian tourists at a surprisingly delightful hotel in the middle of nowhere called the Eagles Palace. There the single most helpful hotel employee I have ever met (ask for Olga) handed me a stack of books and said wistfully how lucky I was to be able to visit the place. The Vatopaidi monastery, along with nineteen others, was built in the tenth century on a thirty-seven-mile-long-by-six-mile-wide peninsula in northeast Greece called Mount Athos. Mount Athos now is severed from the mainland by a long fence, and so the only way onto it is by boat, which gives the peninsula the flavor of an island. Onto this island no women are allowed—no female animals of any kind, in fact, except for cats. The official history ascribes the ban to the desire of the church to honor the Virgin; the unofficial one to the problem of monks hitting on female visitors. The ban has stood for one thousand years.

This explains the high-pitched shrieks the next morning, as the ancient ferry packed with monks and pilgrims pulls away from the docks. Dozens of women gather there to holler at the top of their lungs, but with such good cheer that it is unclear whether they are lamenting or celebrating the fact that they cannot accompany their men. Olga has told me that she was pretty sure I was going to need to hike some part of the way to Vatopaidi, and that the people she has seen off to the holy mountain don't usually carry with them anything so redolent of the modern material world as a wheelie bag. As a result, all I have is an Eagles Palace plastic laundry bag with spare underwear, a toothbrush, and a bottle of Ambien.

The ferry chugs for three hours along a rocky, wooded, but otherwise barren coastline, stopping along the way to drop monks and pilgrims and guest workers at other monasteries. The sight of the first one just takes my breath away. It's not a building but a spectacle: it's as if someone had taken Assisi or Todi or one of the other old central Italian hill towns and plopped it down on the beach, in the middle of nowhere. Unless you know what to expect on Mount Athos—it has been regarded by the Eastern Orthodox Church for more than a millennium as the holiest place on earth, and it enjoyed for much of that time a symbiotic relationship with Byzantine emperors—these places come as a shock. There's nothing modest about them; they are grand and complicated and ornate and obviously in some sort of competition with one another. In the old days, pirates routinely plundered them, and you can see why: it would be almost shameful not to, for a pirate.

There are many places in the world where you

can get away with not speaking Greek. Athens is one of them; the Mount Athos ferryboat is not. I am saved by an English-speaking young man who, to my untrained eye, looks like any other monk: long dark robes, long dark shaggy beard, fog of unfriendliness which, once penetrated, evaporates. He spots me using a map with thumbnail sketches of the monasteries and trying to determine where the hell I am meant to get off the boat: he introduces himself. His name is Cesar; he's Romanian, the son of a counter-espionage secret policeman in the nightmarish regime of Nicolae Ceauşescu. Somehow he has retained his sense of humor, which counts as some kind of miracle. He explains that if I knew anything about anything I would know that he was no monk, merely another Romanian priest on holiday. He's traveled from Bucharest, with two enormous trunks on wheelies, to spend his summer vacation in one of the monasteries. Three months living on bread and water with no women in sight is his idea of a vacation. The world outside Mount Athos he finds somehow lacking.

Cesar draws me a little map to use to get to Vatopaidi and gives me a more general lay of the land. The mere fact that I don't have a beard will expose me as a not terribly holy man, he explains, if my mauve Brooks Brothers shirt doesn't do it first. "But they are used to having visitors," he said, "so it shouldn't be a problem." Then he pauses and asks, "But what is your religion?"

"I don't have one."

"But you believe in God?"

"No."

He thinks this over.

"Then I'm pretty sure they can't let you in."

He lets the thought sink in. "On the other hand, how much worse could it get for you?" he says, and chuckles.

An hour later I'm walking off the ferry holding nothing but the Eagles Palace hotel laundry bag and Cesar's little map, and he's still repeating his own punch line—"How much worse could it get for you?"—and laughing more loudly each time.

The monk who meets me at Vatopaidi's front gate glances at the laundry bag and hands me a form to fill in. An hour later, having pretended to settle into my surprisingly comfortable cell, I'm carried by a river of bearded monks through the church door. Fearing that I might be tossed out of the monastery before I got a sense of the place, I do what I can to fit in. I follow the monks into their church; I light candles and jam them into a tiny sandpit; I cross myself incessantly; I air-kiss the icons. No one seems to care one way or the other about the obviously not-Greek guy in the mauve Brooks Brothers shirt, though right through the service a fat young monk who looks a bit like Jack Black glares at me, as if I was neglecting some critical piece of instruction.

Otherwise the experience was sensational, to be recommended to anyone looking for a taste of tenth-century life. Beneath titanic polished golden chandeliers, and surrounded by freshly cleaned icons, the monks sang; the monks chanted; the monks vanished behind screens to utter strange incantations; the monks shook what sounded like sleigh bells; the monks floated by waving thuribles, leaving in their wake smoke and the ancient odor of incense. Every word that was said and sung and chanted was biblical Greek (it seemed to have something to do with Jesus Christ), but I nodded right along anyway. I stood when they stood, and sat when they sat: up and down we went like pogo sticks, for hours. The effect of the whole thing was heightened by the monks' magnificently wild beards. Even when left to nature, beards do not all grow in the same way. There are types: the hopelessly porous mass of fuzz; the Osama bin Laden/Assyrian-king trowel; the Karl Marx bird's nest. A surprising number of the monks resembled the Most Interesting Man in the World from the Dos Equis commercial. ("His beard alone has experienced more than a lesser man's entire body.")

The Vatopaidi monks have a reputation for knowing a lot more about you than you imagine they do, and for sensing what they do not know.

A woman who runs one of the big Greek shipping firms told me over dinner in Athens that she had found herself seated on a flight not long ago beside Father Ephraim, the abbot of Vatopaidi (business class). "It was a *very* strange experience," she said. "He knew nothing about me, but he guessed everything. My marriage. How I felt about my work. I felt that he completely knew me." Inside their church I doubted their powers—in the middle of a great national scandal they have allowed a writer, albeit one who has not formally announced himself, to show up, bunk down, and poke around their monastery without asking the first question.

But coming out of the church I finally get seized: a roundish monk with a salt-and-pepper beard and skin the color of a brown olive corners me. He introduces himself as Father Arsenios.

FOR MOST OF the 1980s and 1990s, Greek interest rates had run a full 10 percent higher than German ones, as Greeks were regarded as far less likely to repay a loan. There was no consumer credit in Greece: Greeks didn't have credit cards. Greeks didn't usually have mortgage loans, either. Of course, Greece wanted to be treated, by the financial markets, like a properly functioning Northern European country. In the late 1990s they saw their chance: get rid of their own currency and adopt the euro. To do this they needed to meet certain national targets, to prove that they were capable of good European citizenship—that they would not, in the end, run up debts that other countries in the euro area would be forced to repay. In particular they needed to show budget deficits under 3 percent of their gross domestic product, and inflation running at roughly German levels. In 2000, after a flurry of statistical manipulation, Greece hit the targets. To lower the budget deficit the Greek government moved all sorts of expenses (pensions, defense expenditures) off the books. To lower Greek inflation the government did things like freeze prices for electricity and water and other government-supplied goods, and cut taxes on gas, alcohol, and tobacco. Greek government statisticians did things like remove (high-priced) tomatoes from the consumer price index on the day inflation was measured. "We went to see the guy who created all these numbers," a former Wall Street analyst of European economies told me. "We could not stop laughing. He explained how he took out the lemons and put in the oranges. There was a lot of massaging of the index."

Which is to say that even at the time, some observers noted that Greek numbers never seemed to add up. A former IMF official turned economic adviser to former Greek prime minister Konstantinos Mitsotakis turned Salomon

Brothers analyst named Miranda Xafa pointed out in 1998 that if you added up all the Greek budget deficits over the previous fifteen years they amounted to only half the Greek debt. That is, the amount of money the Greek government had borrowed to fund its operations was twice its declared shortfalls. "At Salomon we used to call [the then head of the Greek National Statistical Service] 'the Magician,' " says Xafa, "because of his ability to magically make inflation, the deficit, and the debt disappear."

In 2001, Greece entered the European Monetary Union, swapped the drachma for the euro, and acquired for its debt an implicit European (read German) guarantee. Greeks could now borrow long-term funds at roughly the same rate as Germans—not 18 percent but 5 percent. To remain in the euro zone, they were meant, in theory, to maintain budget deficits below 3 percent of GDP; in practice, all they had to do was cook the books to show that they were hitting the targets. Here, in 2001, entered Goldman Sachs, which engaged in a series of apparently legal but nonetheless repellent deals designed to hide the Greek government's true level of indebtedness. For these trades Goldman Sachs— which, in effect, handed Greece a $1 billion loan—carved out a reported $300 million in fees. The machine that enabled Greece to borrow and spend at will was analogous to the machine created to launder the credit of the American subprime borrower—and the role of the American investment banker in the machine was the same. The investment bankers also taught the Greek government officials how to securitize future receipts from the national lottery, highway tolls, airport landing fees, and even funds granted to the country by the European Union. Any future stream of income that could be identified was sold for cash up front and spent. As anyone with a brain must have known, the Greeks would be able to disguise their true financial state for only as long as (a) lenders assumed that a loan to Greece was as good as guaranteed by the European Union (read Germany), and (b) no one outside of Greece paid very much attention. Inside Greece there was no market for whistle-blowing, as basically everyone was in on the racket.

That changed on October 4, 2009, when the Greek government turned over. A scandal felled the government of Prime Minister Kostas Karamanlis and sent him packing, which perhaps is not surprising. What's surprising was the nature of the scandal. In late 2008, news broke that Vatopaidi had somehow acquired a fairly worthless lake and swapped it for far more valuable government-owned land. How the monks did this was unclear—paid some enormous bribe to some government official, it was assumed. No bribe could be found, however. It didn't matter: the furor that followed drove Greek politics for the next year. The Vatopaidi scandal registered in Greek public opinion like nothing in memory. "We've never seen a movement in the polls like we saw after the scandal broke," the editor of one of Greece's leading newspapers told me. "Without Vatopaidi, Karamanlis is still the prime minister, and everything is still going on as it was before." Dimitri Contominas, the billionaire creator of a Greek life-insurance company and, as it happens, owner of the TV station that broke the Vatopaidi scandal, put it to me more bluntly: "The Vatopaidi monks brought George Papandreou to power."

After the new party (the supposedly socialist Pasok) replaced the old party (the supposedly conservative New Democracy), it found so much less money in the government's coffers than it had expected that it decided there was no choice but to come clean. The prime minister announced that Greece's budget deficits had been badly understated—and that it was going to take some time to nail down the numbers. Pension funds and global bond funds and other sorts who buy Greek bonds, having seen several big American and British banks go belly-up, and knowing the fragile state of a lot of European banks, panicked. The new, higher interest rates Greece was forced to pay left the country—which needed to borrow vast sums to fund its operations—more or less bankrupt. In came the IMF to examine the Greek books more closely; out went whatever tiny shred of credibility the Greeks had left. "How in the hell is it possible for a member of the euro area to say the deficit was 3 percent of GDP when it was really 15 percent?" a senior IMF official asks. "How could you possibly do something like that?"

Just now the global financial system is consumed with the question of whether the Greeks will default on their debts. At times it seems as if it is the only question that matters, for if Greece walks away from $400 billion in debt, then the European banks that lent the money will go down, and other countries now flirting with bankruptcy (Spain, Portugal) might easily follow. But this question of whether Greece will repay its debts is really a question of whether Greece will change its culture, and that will happen only if Greeks want to change. I am told fifty times if I am told once that what Greeks care about is "justice," and what really boils the Greek blood is the feeling of unfairness. Obviously this distinguishes them from no human being on the planet, and ignores what's interesting: exactly what a Greek finds unfair. It's clearly not the corruption of their political system. It's not cheating on their taxes, or taking small bribes in their service to the state. No: what bothers them is when some outside party—someone clearly different from themselves, with motives apart from narrow and easily understood self-interest—comes in and exploits the corruption of their system. Enter the monks.

Among the first moves made by the new minister of finance was to file a lawsuit against the Vatopaidi monastery, demanding the return of government property *and* damages. Among the first acts of the new parliament was to open a second investigation of the Vatopaidi affair, to finally nail down exactly how the monks got their sweet deal. The one public official who has been strung up—he's had his passport taken away and remains free only because he posted a bail of 400,000 euros—is an assistant to the former prime minister, Giannis Angelou, who stands accused of helping these monks.

In a society that has endured something like total moral collapse, its monks had somehow become the single universally acceptable target of moral outrage. Every right-thinking Greek citizen is still furious with them and those who helped them, and yet no one knows exactly what they did, or why.

FATHER ARSENIOS LOOKS to be in his late fifties—though who knows, as their beards cause them all to look twenty years older. He's about as famous as you can get, for a monk: everyone in Athens knows who he is. Mr. Inside, the consummate number two, the CFO, the real brains of the operation. "If they put Arsenios in charge of the government real-estate portfolio," a prominent Greek real estate agent said to me, "this country would be *Dubai*. Before the crisis." If you are kindly disposed to these monks, Father Arsenios is the trusted assistant who makes possible the miraculous abbacy of Father Ephraim. If you are not, he's Jeff Skilling to Ephraim's Kenneth Lay.

I tell him who I am and what I do—and also that I have spent the past few days interviewing political types in Athens. He smiles, genuinely: he's pleased I've come! "The politicians all used to come here," he says, "but because of our scandal they don't now. They are afraid of being seen with us!"

He escorts me into the dining hall and plants me at what appears to be the pilgrim's table of honor, right next to the table filled with the top monks. Father Ephraim heads that table, with Arsenios in shouting distance.

Most of what the monks eat they grow themselves within a short walk of the dining hall. Crude silver bowls contain raw, uncut onions, green beans, cucumbers, tomatoes, and beets. Another bowl holds bread baked by the monks, from their own wheat. There's a pitcher of water and, for dessert, a soupy orange sherbet-like substance and dark honeycomb recently plundered from some beehive. And that's pretty much it. If it were a restaurant in Berkeley, people would revel in the glorious self-righteousness of eating the locally grown; here the food just seems plain. The monks eat like fashion models before a shoot. Twice a day four days a week, and once a day for three: eleven meals, all of them more or less like this. Which raises an obvious question: Why are some of them fat? Most of them—maybe 100 out of the 110 now in residence—resemble their diet. Beyond thin: *narrow*. But a handful, including the two bosses, have an ampleness to them that cannot be explained by eleven helpings of raw onion and cucumber, no matter how much honeycomb they chew through.

After dinner the monks return to church, where they will remain chanting and singing and crossing and spraying incense until one in the morning. Arsenios grabs me and takes me for a walk. We pass Byzantine chapels and climb Byzantine stairs until we arrive at a door in a long Byzantine hall freshly painted but otherwise antique: his office. On the desk are two computers; behind it a brand-new fax machine-cum-printer; on top of it a cell phone and a Costco-size tub of vitamin C pills. The walls and floor gleam like new. The cabinets exhibit row upon row of three-ring binders. The only sign that this isn't a business office circa 2010 is a single icon over the desk. Apart from that, if you put this office side by side with the office of Greece's minister of finance and asked which one housed the monk, this wouldn't be it.

"There is more of a spiritual thirst today," he says, when I ask him why his monastery has attracted so many important business and political people. "Twenty or thirty years ago they taught that science will solve all problems. There are so many material things and they are not satisfying. People have gotten tired of material pleasures. Of material things. And they realize they cannot really find success in these things." And with that he picks up the phone and orders drinks and dessert. Moments later a silver tray arrives, bearing pastries and glasses of what appears to be crème de menthe.

Thus began what became a three-hour encounter. I'd ask simple questions—Why on earth would anyone become a monk? How do you handle life without women? How do people who spend ten hours a day in church find time to create real estate empires? Where did you get the crème de menthe?—and he would answer in twenty-minute-long parables in which there would be, somewhere, a simple answer. (For example: "I believe there are many more beautiful things than sex.") As he told his stories he waved and jumped around and smiled and laughed: if Father Arsenios feels guilty about anything, he has a rare talent for hiding it. Like a lot of people who come to Vatopaidi, I suppose, I was less than perfectly sure what I was after. I wanted to see if it felt like a front for a commercial empire (it doesn't) and if the monks seemed insincere (hardly). But I also wondered how a bunch of odd-looking guys who had walked away from the material world had such a knack for getting their way in it: How on earth do monks, of all people, wind up as Greece's best shot at a Harvard Business School case study?

After about two hours I work up the nerve to ask him. To my surprise he takes me seriously. He points to a sign he has tacked up on one of his cabinets, and translates it from the Greek: The smart person accepts. The idiot insists.

He got it, he says, on one of his business trips to the Ministry of Tourism. "This is the secret of success for anywhere in the world, not just the monastery," he says, and then goes on to describe pretty much word for word the first rule of improvisational comedy, or for that matter any successful collaborative enterprise. Take whatever is thrown at you and build upon it. "Yes . . . and" rather than "No . . . but." "The idiot is bound by his pride," he says. "It always has to be *his* way. This is also true of the person who is deceptive or doing things wrong: he always tries to justify himself. A person who is bright in regard to his spiritual life is humble. He accepts what others tell him—criticism, ideas—and he works with them."

I notice now that his windows open upon a balcony overlooking the Aegean Sea. The monks are not permitted to swim in it; why, I never asked. Just like them, though, to build a beach house and then ban the beach. I notice, also, that I am the only one who has eaten the pastries and drunk the crème de menthe. It occurs to me that I may have just failed some sort of test of my ability to handle temptation.

"The whole government says they are angry at us," he says, "but we have nothing. We work for others. The Greek newspapers, they call us a corporation. But I ask you, Michael, what company has lasted for a thousand years?"

At that moment, out of nowhere, Father Ephraim walks in. Round, with rosy cheeks and a white beard, he is more or less the spitting image of Santa Claus. He even has a twinkle in his eye. A few months before, he'd been hauled before the Greek parliament to testify. One of his interrogators said that the Greek government had acted with unusual efficiency when it swapped Vatopaidi's lake for the Ministry of Agriculture's commercial properties. He asked Ephraim how he had done it.

"Don't you believe in miracles?" Ephraim had said.

"I'm beginning to," said the Greek MP.

When we are introduced, Ephraim clasps my hand and holds it for a very long time. It crosses my mind that he is about to ask me what I want for Christmas. Instead he says, "What is your faith?" "Episcopalian," I cough out. He nods; he calibrates: it could be worse; it probably is worse. "You are married?" he asks. "Yes." "You have children?" I nod; he calibrates: *I can work with this*. He asks for their names . . .

THE SECOND PARLIAMENTARY inquiry into the Vatopaidi affair is still gathering steam, and you never know what it may turn up. But the main facts of the case are not in dispute; the main question left to answer is the motives of the monks and the public servants who helped them. In the late 1980s, Vatopaidi was a complete ruin—a rubble of stones overrun with rats. The frescoes were black. The icons went uncared for. The place had a dozen monks roaming around its ancient stones, but they were autonomous and disorganized. In church jargon they worshipped idiorrhythmically—which is another way of saying that in their quest for spiritual satisfaction it was every man for himself. No one was in charge; they had no collective purpose. Their relationship to their monastery, in other words, was a lot like the relationship of the Greek citizen to his state.

That changed in the early 1990s, when a group of energetic young Greek Cypriot monks from another part of Athos, led by Father Ephraim, saw a rebuilding opportunity: a fantastic natural asset that had been terribly mismanaged. Ephraim set about raising the money to restore Vatopaidi to its former glory. He dunned the European Union for cultural funds. He mingled with rich Greek businessmen in need of forgiveness. He cultivated friendships with important Greek politicians. In all of this he exhibited incredible chutzpah. For instance, after a famous Spanish singer visited and took an interest in Vatopaidi, he parlayed the interest into an audience with government officials from Spain. They were told a horrible injustice had occurred: in the fourteenth century a band of Catalan mercenaries, upset with the Byzantine emperor, had sacked Vatopaidi and caused much damage. The monastery received $240,000 from the government officials.

Clearly one part of Ephraim's strategy was to return Vatopaidi to what it had been for much of the Byzantine Empire: a monastery with global reach. This, too, distinguished it from the country it happened to be inside. Despite its entry into the European Union, Greece has remained a closed economy; it's impossible to put one finger on the source of all the country's troubles, but if you laid a hand on them, one finger would touch its insularity. All sorts of things that might be more efficiently done by other people they do themselves; all sorts of interactions with other countries that they might profitably engage in simply do not occur. In the general picture the Vatopaidi monastery was a stunning exception: it cultivated relations with the outside world. Most famously, until scandal hit, Prince Charles had visited three summers in a row, and stayed for a week each visit.

Relationships with the rich and famous were essential in Vatopaidi's pursuit of government grants and reparations for sackings, but also for the third prong of its new management's strategy: real estate. By far the smartest thing Father Ephraim had done was go rummaging around in an old tower where they kept the Byzantine manuscripts, untouched for decades. Over the centuries Byzantine emperors and other rulers had deeded to Vatopaidi various tracts of land, mainly in modern-day Greece and Turkey. In the years before Ephraim arrived, the Greek government had clawed back much of this property, but there remained a title, bestowed in the fourteenth century by Emperor John V Palaiologos, to a lake in northern Greece.

By the time Ephraim discovered the deed to the lake in Vatopaidi's vaults, it had been designated a nature preserve by the Greek government. Then, in 1998, suddenly it wasn't: someone had allowed the designation to lapse. Shortly thereafter, the monks were granted full title to the lake.

Back in Athens, I tracked down Peter Doukas, the official inside the Ministry of Finance first accosted by the Vatopaidi monks. Doukas now finds himself at the center of the two parliamentary investigations, but he had become, oddly, the one person in government willing to speak openly about what had happened. (He was by birth not an Athenian but a Spartan—but perhaps that's another story.) Unlike most of the people in the Greek government, Doukas wasn't a lifer but a guy who had made his fortune in the private sector, inside and outside of Greece, and then, in 2004, at the request of the prime minister, had taken a post in the Finance Ministry. He was then fifty-two years old and had spent most of his career as a banker with Citigroup in New York. He was tall and blond and loud and blunt and funny. It was Doukas who was responsible for the very existence of long-term Greek-government debt. Back when interest rates were low, and no one saw any risk in lending money to the Greek government, he talked his superiors into issuing forty- and fifty-year bonds. Afterwards the Greek newspapers ran headlines attacking him (DOUKAS MORTGAGES OUR CHILDREN'S FUTURE), but it was a very bright thing to have done. The $18 billion of long-term bonds now trade at 50 cents on the dollar—which is to say that the Greek government could buy them back on the open market. "I created a nine-billion-dollar trading profit for them," says Doukas, laughing. "They should give me a bonus!"

Not long after Doukas began his new job, two monks showed up unannounced in his Finance Ministry office. One was Father Ephraim, of whom Doukas had heard; the other, unknown to Doukas but clearly the sharp end of the operation, a fellow named Father Arsenios. They owned this lake, they said, and they wanted the Ministry of Finance to pay them cash for it. "Someone had given them full title to the lake," says Doukas. "What they wanted now was to monetize it. They came to me and said, 'Can you buy us out?'" Before the meeting, Doukas sensed, they had done a great deal of homework. "Before they come to you they know *a lot* about you—your wife, your parents, the extent of your religious beliefs," he said. "The first thing they asked me was if I wanted them to take my confession." Doukas decided that it would be unwise to tell the monks his secrets. Instead he told them he would not give them money for their lake—which he still didn't see how exactly they had come to own. "They seemed to think I had all this money to spend," says Doukas. "I said, 'Listen, contrary to popular opinion, there is no money in the Finance Ministry.' And they said, 'Okay, if you cannot buy us out, why can't you give us some of your pieces of land?'"

This turned out to be the winning strategy: exchanging the lake, which generated no rents, for government-owned properties that did. Somehow the monks convinced government officials that the land around the lake was worth far more than the 55 million euros an independent appraiser later assessed its value as, and then used that higher valuation to ask for 1 billion euros' worth of government property. Doukas declined to give them any of the roughly 250 billion euros' worth controlled by the Ministry of Finance. ("No fucking way I'm doing that," he says he told them.) The monks went to the source of the next most valuable land—farmlands and forests controlled by the Ministry of Agriculture. Doukas recalls, "I get a call from the minister of agriculture saying, 'We're trading them all this land, but it's not enough. Why don't you throw in some of your pieces of land, too?'" After Doukas declined, he received another call—this one from the prime minister's office. Still he said no. Next he receives this piece of paper saying he's giving the monks government land, and all he needs to do is sign it. "I said, 'Fuck you, I'm not signing it.'"

And he didn't—at least not in its original form. But the prime minister's office pressed him; the monks, it seemed to Doukas, had some kind of hold on the prime minister's chief of staff. That fellow, Giannis Angelou, had come to know the monks a few years before, just after he had been diagnosed with a life-threatening illness. The monks prayed for him; he didn't die, but instead made a miraculous recovery. He had, however, given them his confession.

By now Doukas thought of these monks less as simple con men than as the savviest businessmen he had ever dealt with. "I told them they should be running the Ministry of Finance," he says. "They didn't disagree." In the end, under pressure from his boss, Doukas signed two pieces of paper. The first agreed not to challenge the monks' ownership of the lake; the second made possible the land exchange. It did not give the monks rights to any lands from the Finance Ministry, but, by agreeing to accept their lake into the Ministry of Finance's real estate portfolio, Doukas enabled their deal with the minister of agriculture. In exchange for their lake the monks received seventy-three different government properties, including what had formerly been the gymnastics center for the 2004 Olympics— which, like much of what the Greek government built for the Olympic Games, was now empty and abandoned space. And that, Doukas assumed, was that. "You figure they are holy people," he says. "Maybe they want to use it to create an orphanage."

What they wanted to create, as it turned out, was a commercial real estate empire. They began by persuading the Greek government to do something it seldom did: to rezone a lot of noncommercial property for commercial purposes. Above and beyond the lands they received in their swap—which the Greek parliament subsequently estimated to be worth a billion euros—the monks, all by themselves, were getting 100 percent financing to buy commercial buildings in Athens and to develop the properties they had acquired. The former Olympics gymnastics center was to become a fancy private hospital—with which the monks obviously enjoyed a certain synergy. Then, with the help of a Greek banker, the monks drew up plans for something to be called the Vatopaidi Real Estate Fund. Investors in the fund would, in effect, buy the monks out of the properties given to them by the government. And the monks would use the money to restore their monastery to its former glory.

From an ancient deed to a worthless lake the two monks had spun what the Greek newspapers were claiming, depending on the newspaper, to be a fortune of anywhere from tens of millions to many billions of dollars. But the truth was that no one knew the full extent of the monks' financial holdings; indeed, one of the criticisms of the first parliamentary investigation was that it had failed to lay hands on everything the monks owned. On the theory that if you want to know what rich people are really worth you are far better off asking other rich people—as opposed to, say, journalists—I polled a random sample of several rich Greeks who had made their fortune in real estate or finance. They put the monks' real estate and financial assets at less than $2 billion but more than $1 billion—up from zero since the new management took over. And the business had started with nothing to sell but forgiveness.

The monks didn't finish with church until one in the morning. Normally, Father Arsenios explained, they would be up and at it all over again at four. On Sunday they give themselves a break and start at six. Throw in another eight hours a day working the gardens, or washing dishes, or manufacturing crème de menthe, and you can see how one man's idea of heaven might be another's of hell. The bosses of the operation, Fathers Ephraim and Arsenios, escape this grueling regime roughly five days a month; otherwise this is the life they lead. "Most people in Greece have this image of the abbot as a hustler," another monk, named Father Matthew, from Wisconsin, says to me in a moment of what I take to be candor. "Everyone in Greece is convinced that the abbot and Father Arsenios have their secret bank accounts. It's completely mad if you think about it. What are they going to do with it? They don't take a week off and go to the Caribbean. The abbot lives in a cell. It's a nice cell. But he's still a monk. And he *hates* leaving the monastery."

The knowledge that I am meant to be back in the church at six in the morning makes it more, not less, difficult to sleep, and I'm out of bed by five. Perfect silence: it's so rare to hear nothing that it takes a moment to identify the absence. Cupolas, chimneys, towers, and Greek crosses punctuate the gray sky. Also a pair of idle giant cranes: the freezing of the monks' assets has halted restoration of the monastery. At 5:15 come the first rumblings from inside the church; it sounds as if someone is moving around the icon screens, the sweaty backstage preparations before the show. At 5:30 a monk grabs a rope and clangs a church bell. Silence again and then, moments later, from the monk's long dormitory, the *beep beep beep* of electric alarm clocks. Twenty minutes later monks, alone or in pairs, stumble out of their dorm rooms and roll down the cobblestones to their church. It's like watching a factory springing to life in a one-industry town. The only thing missing are the lunch pails.

Three hours later, in the car on the way back to Athens, my cell phone rings. It's Father Matthew. He wants to ask me a favor. *Oh no,* I think, *they've figured out what I'm up to and he's calling to place all sorts of restrictions on what I write*. They had, sort of, but he didn't. The minister of finance insisted on checking his quotes, but the monks just let me run with whatever I had, which is sort of amazing, given the scope of the lawsuits they face. "We have been reading this adviser in the American stock market," says the monk. "His name is Robert Chapman . . ." (I'd never heard of him. He turned out to be the writer of a newsletter about global finance.) His fellow monks, said Father Matthew, were wondering what I thought of Robert Chapman. Whether he was worth listening to . . .

**THE DAY BEFORE** I left Greece the Greek parliament debated and voted on a bill to raise the retirement age, reduce government pensions, and otherwise reduce the spoils of public-sector life. ("I'm all for reducing the number of public-sector employees," an IMF investigator had said to me. "But how do you do that if you don't know how many there are to start with?") Prime Minister Papandreou presented this bill, as he has presented everything since he discovered the hole in the books, not as his own idea but as a nonnegotiable demand of the IMF's. The general idea seems to be that while the Greek people will never listen to any internal call for sacrifice they might listen to calls from outside. That is, they no longer really even want to govern themselves.

Thousands upon thousands of government

employees take to the streets to protest the bill. Here is Greece's version of the Tea Party: tax collectors on the take, public-school teachers who don't really teach, well-paid employees of bankrupt state railroads whose trains never run on time, state hospital workers bribed to buy overpriced supplies. Here they are, and here we are: a nation of people looking for anyone to blame but themselves. The Greek public-sector employees assemble themselves into units that resemble army platoons. In the middle of each unit are two or three rows of young men wielding truncheons disguised as flagpoles. Ski masks and gas masks dangle from their belts so that they can still fight after the inevitable tear gas. "The deputy prime minister has told us that they are looking to have at least one death," a prominent former Greek minister had told me. "They want some blood." Two months earlier, on May 5, during the first of these protest marches, the mob offered a glimpse of what it was capable of. Seeing people working at a branch of the Marfin Bank, young men hurled Molotov cocktails inside and tossed gasoline on top of the flames, barring the exit. Most of the Marfin Bank's employees escaped from the roof, but the fire killed three workers, including a young woman four months pregnant. As they died, Greeks in the streets screamed at them that it served them right, for having the audacity to work. The events took place in full view of the Greek police, and yet the police made no arrests.

As on other days, the protesters have effectively shut down the country. The air-traffic controllers have also gone on strike and closed the airport. At the port of Piraeus, the mob prevents cruise-ship passengers from going ashore and shopping. At the height of the tourist season the tourist dollars this place so desperately needs are effectively blocked from getting into the country. Any private-sector employee who does not skip work in sympathy is in danger. All over Athens shops and restaurants close; so, for that matter, does the Acropolis.

The lead group assembles in the middle of a wide boulevard a few yards from the burned and gutted bank branch. That they burned a bank is, under the circumstances, incredible. If there were any justice in the world the Greek bankers would be in the streets marching to protest the morals of the ordinary Greek citizen. The Marfin Bank's marble stoop has been turned into a sad shrine: a stack of stuffed animals for the unborn child, a few pictures of monks, a sign with a quote from the ancient orator Isocrates: "Democracy destroys itself because it abuses its right to freedom and equality. Because it teaches its citizens to consider audacity as a right, lawlessness as a freedom, abrasive speech as equality, and anarchy as progress." At the other

115

end of the street a phalanx of riot police stand, shields together, like Spartan warriors. Behind them is the Parliament building; inside, the debate presumably rages, though what is being said and done is a mystery, as the Greek journalists aren't working, either. The crowd begins to chant and march toward the vastly outnumbered police: the police stiffen. It's one of those moments when it feels as if anything might happen. Really, it's just a question of which way people jump.

That's how it feels in the financial markets, too. The question everyone wants an answer to is: Will Greece default? There's a school of thought that says they have no choice: the very measures the government imposes to cut costs and raise revenues will cause what is left of the productive economy to flee the country. The taxes are lower in Bulgaria, the workers more pliable in Romania. But there's a second, more interesting, question: Even if it is technically possible for these people to repay their debts, live within their means, and return to good standing inside the European Union, do they have the inner resources to do it? Or have they so lost their ability to feel connected to anything outside their small worlds that they would rather just shed the obligations? On the face of it, defaulting on their debts and walking away would seem a mad act: all Greek banks would instantly go bankrupt, the country

116

would have no ability to pay for the many necessities it imports (oil, for instance), and the government would be punished for many years in the form of much higher interest rates, if and when it was allowed to borrow again. But the place does not behave as a collective; it lacks the monks' instincts. It behaves as a collection of atomized particles, each of which has grown accustomed to pursuing its own interest at the expense of the common good. There's no question that the government is resolved to at least try to re-create Greek civic life. The only question is: Can such a thing, once lost, ever be re-created?

# III

## IRELAND'S
## ORIGINAL SIN

When I flew to Dublin in early November 2010 the Irish government was busy helping the Irish people come to terms with their loss. It had been two years since a handful of Irish politicians and bankers had decided to guarantee all the debts of the biggest Irish banks, but the people were only now getting their minds around what that meant for them. The numbers were breathtaking. A single bank, Anglo Irish, which, two years before, the Irish government claimed was suffering from a "liquidity problem," confessed to losses of 34 billion euros. To get a sense of how "34 billion euros" sounds to Irish ears, an American thinking in dollars needs to multiply it by roughly one hundred: $3.4 trillion. And that was for a *single bank*. As the sum total of loans made by Anglo Irish Bank, most of it to Irish property developers, was only 72 billion euros, the bank had lost nearly half of every dollar it invested.

The two other big Irish banks, Bank of Ireland and, especially, Allied Irish Banks (AIB), remained Ireland's dirty little secret. Both older than Ireland itself (the Bank of Ireland was founded in 1783; Allied Irish was formed in a merger of three banks founded in the 1800s), both were now also obviously bust. The Irish government owned most of the two ancient banks, but revealed less about them than they had about Anglo Irish. As they had lent vast sums not only to Irish property developers but also to Irish home buyers, their losses were obviously vast—and similar in spirit to the losses at the upstart Anglo Irish. Even in an era when capitalists went out of their way to destroy capitalism, the Irish bankers had set some kind of record for destruction. Theo Phanos, whose London hedge fund has interests in Ireland, says that "Anglo Irish was probably the world's worst bank. Even worse than the Icelandic banks."

IRELAND'S FINANCIAL DISASTER shared some things in common with Iceland's. It was created by the sort of men who ignore their wives' suggestions that maybe they should stop and ask for directions, for instance. But while the Icelandic male used foreign money to conquer foreign places—trophy companies in Britain, chunks of Scandinavia—the Irish male used foreign money to conquer Ireland. Left alone in a dark room with a pile of money, the Irish decided what they really wanted to do with it was buy Ireland. *From each other.* An Irish economist named Morgan Kelly, whose estimates of Irish bank losses have been the most prescient, has made a back-of-the-envelope calculation that puts the property-related losses of all Irish banks at roughly 106 billion euros. (Think $10.6 trillion.) At the rate money flows into the Irish treasury, Irish bank losses alone would absorb every penny of Irish taxes for the next four years.

In recognition of the spectacular losses, the entire Irish economy has almost dutifully collapsed. When you fly into Dublin you are traveling, for the first time in fifteen years, against the traffic. The Irish are once again leaving Ireland, along with hordes of migrant workers. In late 2006 the unemployment rate stood at a bit more than 4 percent; now it's 14 percent, and climbing toward rates not experienced since the mid-1980s. Just a few years ago Ireland was able to borrow money more cheaply than Germany; now, if it can borrow at all, it will be charged interest rates 6 percent higher than Germany, another echo of a distant past. The Irish budget deficit—in 2007 the country had a budget surplus—is now 32 percent of its GDP, the highest by far in the history of the euro zone. Professional credit analyst firms now judge Ireland the third most likely country in the world to default. Not quite as risky for the global investor as Venezuela, perhaps, but riskier than Iraq. Distinctly third world, in any case.

Yet when I arrived, Irish politics had a frozen-in-time quality. In Iceland, the business-friendly conservative party had been quickly tossed out of power, and the women had booted the alpha males out of the banks and government. In Greece the corrupt, business-friendly, every-Greek-for-himself conservative party was also given the heave-ho, and the new government is attempting to create a sense of collective purpose, or at any rate persuade the citizens to quit cheating on their taxes. (The new Greek prime minister is not merely upstanding but barely Greek.) Ireland was the first European country to watch its entire banking system fail, and yet its business-friendly conservative party, Fianna Fáil (pronounced "Feena Foil"), remained in office up until February 2011. There's no Tea Party movement, no Glenn Beck, no serious protests of any kind. The only obvious change in the country's politics has been the role played by foreigners. The new bank regulator, an Englishman, came from Bermuda. The Irish government and Irish banks are crawling with American investment bankers and Australian management consultants and faceless Euro-officials, referred to inside the Department of Finance simply as "the Germans." Walk the streets at night and, through restaurant windows, you see important-looking men in suits, dining alone, studying important-looking papers. In some new and strange way Dublin was now an occupied city: Hanoi, circa 1950. "The problem with Ireland is that you're not allowed to work with Irish people anymore," an Irish property developer told me. He was finding it difficult to escape hundreds of millions of euros in debt he would never be able to repay.

Ireland's regress is especially unsettling because of the questions it raises about Ireland's former progress: even now no one is quite sure why the Irish did so well for themselves in the first place. Between 1845 and 1852 the country experienced the single greatest loss of population in world history: in a nation of 8 million, 1.5 million people left. Another million Irish people starved to death, or died from the effects of hunger. Inside of a decade the nation went from being among the most densely populated in Europe to one of the least. The founding of the Irish state in 1922 might have offered some economic hope—they now had their own central bank, their own economic policies—but right up until the end of the 1980s the Irish had failed to do what economists expected them to do: catch up with their neighbors' standard of living. As recently as the 1980s 1 million Irish people, in a nation of a mere 3.2 million, lived below the poverty line.

WHAT HAS OCCURRED in Ireland since then is without precedent in economic history. By the start of the new millennium the Irish poverty rate was under 6 percent, and Ireland was the second richest country in the world, according to the Bank of Ireland. How did that happen? A bright young Irishman who got himself hired by Bear Stearns in the late 1990s and went off to New York or London for five years returned feeling *poor*. For the better part of the past decade there's been quicker money to be made in Irish real estate than in American investment banking. How did *that* happen? For the first time in history people and money longed to get into Ireland rather than out of it. The most dramatic case in point are the Poles. The Polish government keeps no official statistics on the movement of its workforce, but its Foreign Ministry guesstimates that, since their admission to the European Union, a million Poles have left Poland to work elsewhere—and that, at the peak, in 2006, a quarter of a million of them were in Ireland. For the United States to achieve a proportionally distortive demographic effect it would need to hand green cards to 17.5 million Mexicans.

HOW DID ANY of this happen? There are many theories: the elimination of trade barriers, the decision to grant free public higher education, a low corporate tax rate introduced in the 1980s, which turned Ireland into a tax haven for foreign corporations. Maybe the most intriguing was

124

offered by a pair of demographers at Harvard, David E. Bloom and David Canning, in a 2003 paper called "Contraception and the Celtic Tiger." Bloom and Canning argued that a major cause of the Irish boom was a dramatic increase in the ratio of working-age to non–working-age Irishmen, brought about by a crash in the Irish birthrate. This in turn had been mainly driven by Ireland's decision, in 1979, to legalize birth control. That is, there was an inverse correlation between a nation's fidelity to the Vatican's edicts and its ability to climb out of poverty: out of the slow death of the Irish Catholic Church arose an economic miracle.

The Harvard demographers admitted their theory explained only part of what had happened in Ireland. And at the bottom of the success of the Irish there remains, even now, some mystery. "It appeared like a miraculous beast materializing in a forest clearing," writes the preeminent Irish historian R. F. Foster, "and economists are still not entirely sure why." Not knowing why they were so suddenly so successful, the Irish can perhaps be forgiven for not knowing exactly how successful they were meant to be. They'd gone from being abnormally poor to being abnormally rich without pausing to experience normality. When, in the early 2000s, the financial markets began to offer virtually unlimited credit to all comers—when nations were let into the dark room with the pile of money, and asked what they would like to do with it—the Irish were already in a peculiarly vulnerable state of mind. They'd spent the better part of a decade under something very like a magic spell.

A few months after the spell was broken, the short-term parking lot attendants at Dublin Airport noticed that their daily take had fallen. The lot appeared full; they couldn't understand it; then they noticed the cars never changed. They phoned the Dublin police, who in turn traced the cars to Polish construction workers, who had bought them with money borrowed from the big Irish banks. The migrant workers had ditched the cars and gone home. A few months later the Bank of Ireland sent three collectors to Poland to see what they could get back, but they had no luck. The Poles were untraceable. But for their cars in the short-term parking lot, they might never have existed.

MORGAN KELLY IS a professor of economics at University College Dublin, but he did not, until recently, view it as his business to think much about the economy under his nose. He had written a handful of highly regarded academic papers on topics regarded as abstruse even by academic economists ("The Economic Impact of the Little Ice Age"). "I only stumbled on this catastrophe by accident," he says. "I had never been interested in the Irish economy. The Irish economy is tiny and boring." Kelly saw house prices rising madly, and heard young men in Irish finance to whom he had recently taught economics try to explain why the boom didn't trouble them. And the sight and sound of them troubled him. "Around the middle of 2006 all these former students of ours working for the banks started to appear on TV!" he says. "They were now all bank economists and they were nice guys and all that. And they were all saying the same thing: 'We're going to have a soft landing.'"

The statement struck him as absurd on the face of it: real estate bubbles never end with soft landings. A bubble is inflated by nothing firmer than people's expectations. The moment people cease to believe that house prices will rise forever, they will notice what a terrible long-term investment real estate has become, and flee the market, and the market will *crash*. It was in the nature of real estate booms to end with crashes—just as it was perhaps in Morgan Kelly's nature to assume that if his former students were cast on Irish TV playing the financial experts, something was amiss. "I just started Googling things," he said.

Googling things, Kelly learned that more than a fifth of the Irish workforce was now employed building houses. The Irish construction industry had swollen to become nearly a quarter of Irish

GDP—compared to less than 10 percent or so in a normal economy—and Ireland was building half as many new houses a year as the United Kingdom, which had fifteen times as many people to house. He learned that since 1994 the average price for a Dublin home had risen more than 500 percent. In parts of Dublin rents had fallen to less than 1 percent of the purchase price; that is, you could rent a million-dollar home for less than $833 a month. The investment returns on Irish land were ridiculously low: it made no sense for capital to flow into Ireland to develop more of it. Irish home prices implied an economic growth rate that would leave Ireland, in twenty-five years, three times as rich as the United States. ("A price/earnings ratio above Google's," as Kelly put it.) Where would this growth come from? Since 2000, Irish exports had stalled and the economy had become consumed with building houses and offices and hotels. "Competitiveness didn't matter," says Kelly. "From now on we were going to get rich building houses for each other."

The endless flow of cheap foreign money had teased a new trait out of a nation. "We are sort of a hard, pessimistic people," says Kelly. "We don't look on the bright side." Yet since the year 2000 a lot of people had behaved as if each day would be sunnier than the last. The Irish had discovered optimism.

Their real estate boom had the flavor of a family lie: it was sustainable so long as it went unquestioned and it went unquestioned so long as it appeared sustainable. After all, once the value of Irish real estate came untethered from rents, there was no value for it that couldn't be justified. The 35 million euros Irish entrepreneur Denis O'Brien paid for the impressive manor house on Dublin's Shrewsbury Road sounded like a lot until the real estate developer Sean Dunne's wife paid 58 million euros for the four-thousand-square-foot fixer-upper just down the street. But the minute you compared the rise in prices to real estate booms elsewhere and at other times, you reanchored the conversation; you biffed the narrative. The comparisons that sprung first to Morgan Kelly's mind were with the housing bubbles in the Netherlands in the 1970s (after natural gas was discovered in Holland) and Finland in the 1980s (after oil was found off its coast), but it almost didn't matter which examples he picked: the mere idea that Ireland was not sui generis was the panic-making thought. "There is an iron law of house prices," he wrote. "The more house prices rise relative to income and rents, the more they will subsequently fall."

The problem for Kelly, once he had these thoughts, was what to do with them. "This isn't my day job," he says. "I was working on medieval population theory." By the time I got to him Kelly had angered and alienated the entire Irish business and political establishment, but he was himself neither angry nor alienated, nor even especially public. He's not the pundit type. He works in an office built when Irish higher education was conducted on linoleum floors, beneath fluorescent lights, surrounded by metal bookshelves, and generally felt more like a manufacturing enterprise than a prep school for real estate and finance—and likes it. He's puckish, unrehearsed, and apparently—though in Ireland one wants to be careful about using this word—sane. Though not exactly self-denying, he's clearly more comfortable talking and thinking about subjects other than himself. He spent years in graduate school, and collected a doctorate from Yale, and yet somehow retained an almost childlike curiosity. "I was in this position—sort of being a passenger on this ship," he says. "And you see a big iceberg. And so you go and ask the captain: Is that an iceberg?"

HIS WARNING TO his ship's captain took the form of his first ever newspaper article. Its bottom line: "It is not implausible that [Irish real estate] prices could fall—relative to income—by 40 to 50 percent." At the top of the market, he guessed, prices might fall by a staggering 66 percent. He sent his first piece to the small-circulation *Irish Times*. "It was a whim," he says. "I'm not even sure that I believed what I was saying at the time. My position has always been, 'You can't predict the future.'" As it happened, Kelly had predicted the future, with uncanny accuracy, but to believe what he was saying you had to accept that Ireland was not some weird exception in human financial history. "It had no impact," Kelly says. "The response was general amusement. It was *what will these crazy eggheads come up with next?* sort of stuff."

What the crazy egghead came up with next was the obvious link between Irish real estate prices and Irish banks. After all, the vast majority of the construction was being funded by Irish banks. If the real estate market collapsed, those banks would be on the hook for the losses. "I eventually figured out what was going on," says Kelly. "The average value and number of new mortgages peaked in summer 2006. But lending standards were clearly falling after this." The banks continued to make worse loans, but the people borrowing the money to buy houses were growing wary. "What was happening," says Kelly, "is that a lot of people were getting cold feet." The consequences for Irish banks—and the economy—of the inevitable shift in market sentiment would be catastrophic. The banks' losses would lead them to slash their lending to actually useful businesses. Irish citizens in hock to their banks would cease to spend. And, perhaps worst of all, new construction, on which the entire economy was now premised, would cease.

Kelly wrote his second newspaper article, more or less predicting the collapse of the Irish banks. He pointed out that in the last decade the Irish banks and economy had fundamentally changed. In 1997 the Irish banks were funded entirely by Irish deposits. By 2005 they were getting most of their money from abroad. The small German savers who ultimately supplied the Irish banks with deposits to re-lend in Ireland could take their money back with the click of a computer mouse. Since 2000, lending to construction and real estate had risen from 8 percent of Irish bank lending (the European norm) to 28 percent. One hundred billion euros—or basically the sum total of all Irish bank deposits—had been handed over to Irish commercial property developers. By 2007, Irish banks were lending 40 percent more to property developers alone than they had to the *entire Irish population* seven years earlier. "You probably think that the fact that Irish banks have given speculators €100 billion to gamble with, safe in the knowledge that the taxpayers will cover most losses, is a cause for concern to the Irish Central Bank," Kelly wrote, "but you would be quite wrong."

132

• • •

THIS TIME KELLY sent his piece to a newspaper with a far bigger circulation, the *Irish Independent*. The *Independent*'s editor wrote back to say he found the article offensive and wouldn't publish it. Kelly next turned to the *Sunday Business Post*, but the editor just sat on the piece. The journalists were following the bankers' lead and conflating a positive outlook on real estate prices with a love of country and a commitment to Team Ireland. ("They'd all use this same phrase, 'You're either for us or against us,'" says a prominent Irish bank analyst in Dublin.) Kelly finally went back to the *Irish Times*, which ran his piece in September 2007.

A brief and, to Kelly's way of thinking, pointless controversy ensued. The public relations guy at University College Dublin called the head of the Department of Economics and asked him to find someone to write a learned attack on Kelly's piece. (The department head refused.) A senior executive at Anglo Irish Bank, Matt Moran, called to holler at him. "He went on about how 'the real estate developers who are borrowing from us are so incredibly rich they are only borrowing from us as a favor.' He wanted to argue but we ended up having lunch. This is Ireland, after all." Kelly also received a flurry of worried-sounding messages from financial people in London, but of these he was dismissive.

"I get the impression there's this pool of analysts in the financial markets who spend all day sending scary e-mails to each other." He never found out how much force his little newspaper piece exerted on the minds of people who mattered.

It wasn't until almost exactly one year later, on September 29, 2008, that Morgan Kelly became the startled object of popular interest. The stocks of the three main Irish banks, Anglo Irish, AIB, and Bank of Ireland, had fallen by between a fifth and a half in a single trading session, and a run on Irish bank deposits had started. The Irish government was about to guarantee all the obligations of the six biggest Irish banks. The most plausible explanation for all of this was Morgan Kelly's narrative: that the Irish economy had become a giant Ponzi scheme, and the country was effectively bankrupt. But it was so starkly at odds with the story peddled by Irish government officials and senior Irish bankers— that the banks merely had a "liquidity" problem and that Anglo Irish was "fundamentally sound"—that the two could not be reconciled. The government had a report newly thrown together by Merrill Lynch, which declared that "all of the Irish banks are profitable and well-capitalized." The difference between the official line and Kelly's was too vast to be split. You believed either one or the other, and up until

September 2008, who was going to believe this guy holed up in his office wasting his life writing about the effects of the Little Ice Age on the English population? "I went on TV," says Kelly. "I'll never do it again."

**KELLY'S COLLEAGUES IN** the University College economics department watched his transformation from serious academic to amusing crackpot to disturbingly prescient guru with interest. One was Colm McCarthy, who, in the Irish recession of the late 1980s, played a high-profile role in slashing government spending, and so had experienced the intersection of finance and public opinion. In McCarthy's view the dominant narrative inside the head of the average Irish citizen—and his receptiveness to the story Kelly was telling—changed at roughly ten o'clock in the evening on October 2, 2008. On that night Ireland's bank regulator, a lifelong Central Bank bureaucrat in his sixties named Patrick Neary, came live on national television to be interviewed. The interviewer sounded as if he had just finished reading the collected works of Morgan Kelly. The Irish bank regulator, for his part, looked as if he had been dragged from a hole into which he badly wanted to return. He wore an insecure little mustache, stammered rote answers to questions he had not been asked, and ignored the ones he had been asked.

A banking system is an act of faith: it survives only for as long as people believe it will. Two weeks earlier the collapse of Lehman Brothers had cast doubt on banks everywhere. Ireland's banks had not been managed to withstand doubt; they had been managed to exploit blind faith. Now the Irish people finally caught a glimpse of the guy meant to be safeguarding them: the crazy uncle had been sprung from the family cellar. Here he was, on their televisions, insisting that the Irish banks' problems had nothing whatsoever to do with the loans they'd made . . . when anyone with eyes could see, in the vacant skyscrapers and empty housing estates around them, evidence of bank loans that were not merely bad but insane. "What happened was that everyone in Ireland had the idea that somewhere in Ireland there was a little wise old man who was in charge of the money, and this was the first time they'd ever seen this little man," says McCarthy. "And then they saw him and said, *Who the fuck was that??? Is that the fucking guy who is in charge of the money???* That's when everyone panicked."

ON THE MORNING of the day the Irish government planned to unveil a brutal new budget, I took my seat in the visitors' gallery of the Irish parliament. Beside me sat an aide to Joan Burton, who, as the Labor Party's financial spokesperson, was at the time a fair bet to become Ireland's next minister of finance, the unnatural heir to an unholy mess. Down on the floor the seats are mostly empty, but a handful of politicians, Burton included, discuss what they have been discussing without intermission for the past two years: the nation's financial crisis.

The first thing you notice when you watch the Irish parliament at work is that the politicians say everything twice, once in English and once in Gaelic. As there is no one in Ireland who does not speak English, and a vast majority who do not speak Gaelic, this comes across as a forced gesture that wastes a great deal of time. I ask several Irish politicians if they speak Gaelic, and all offer the same uneasy look and hedgy reply: "Enough to get by." The politicians in Ireland speak Gaelic the way the Real Housewives of Orange County speak French. To ask "Why bother to speak it at all?" is of course to miss the point. Everywhere you turn you see both emulation of the English and a desire, sometimes desperate, for distinction. The Irish insistence on their Irishness—their conceit that they are more devoted to their homeland than the typical citizen of the world—has an element of bluster about it, from top to bottom. At the top are the many very rich Irish people who emit noisy patriotic sounds but arrange officially to live elsewhere so they don't have to pay tax in Ireland; at the bottom, the waves of emigration that define Irish history. The

Irish people and their country are like lovers whose passion is heightened by their suspicion that they will probably wind up leaving each other. Their loud patriotism is a cargo ship for their doubt.

ON THIS DAY, in addition to awaiting word on the budget, the Dáil (pronounced "Doyle"), as the Irish call their House of Representatives, had before it what should have been a controversial piece of business: to vote on whether to call elections to fill its four empty seats. The ruling party, Fianna Fáil, held a slim majority of two seats and, because they are universally believed to have created a financial catastrophe, an approval rating of 15 percent. If the elections were held immediately, they'd have been tossed from power—in itself a radical idea, as they have more or less ruled Ireland since its founding as an independent state, in 1922. Yet they successfully resisted the call to fill the empty seats, right up until they were tossed from power in February 2011.

A bell rings for a vote, and Irish politicians stream in. A few minutes before the vote, the doors to their chamber will be closed and guarded. A politician who is late is a politician who cannot vote. A glass barrier separates the visitors' gallery and the floor: I ask my tour guide about it. "It's not to stop people from throwing things at their government," she says, then goes on to explain. Some years ago an Irish politician came late, after the doors had been locked. He ran up to the visitors' gallery, jumped down from it into the press gallery, ten feet below, and from there rappelled down the wall to the floor. They allowed the vote, but put up the glass barrier. They disapproved of the loophole, but rewarded the guy with the wit to exploit it. This, she claims, is very Irish.

The first to take his seat is Bertie Ahern, the prime minister from June 1997 until May 2008 and Political Perp No. 1. Ahern is known both for a native shrewdness and for saying lots of spectacularly dumb-sounding things that are fun to quote. Tony Blair has credited him with a kind of genius in how he brokered the Northern Ireland peace negotiations; on the other hand, seeking to explain the financial crisis, he actually said, "Lehman's was a world investment bank. They had testicles everywhere." Ahern spent his last days in office denying he'd accepted bribes from property developers, at least in part because so much of what he did in office seemed justified only if he were being paid by property developers to do it. But Bertie Ahern, too, obviously believed in the miracle of Irish real estate. After Morgan Kelly published his article predicting the collapse of the Irish banks, for instance, Ahern famously responded to a question about it by saying,

"Sitting on the sidelines cribbing and moaning is a lost opportunity. I don't know how people who engage in that don't commit suicide."

Now Ahern is just another Irish backbencher, with a hangdog slouch and a face mottled by broken capillaries. To fill the empty hours he's taken a second job writing a sports column for the Rupert Murdoch Sunday tabloid *News of the World*, which just might be the least respectable job in global journalism.* Ahern's star, such as it was, has fallen. When the Irish land boom flipped from miracle to catastrophe, a lot of important people's status, along with perhaps their sense of themselves, flipped with it. An Irish stockbroker has told me that many of the former bankers, some of whom he counts as clients, "actually physically look different." He'd just seen the former CEO of Allied Irish Banks, Eugene Sheehy, in a restaurant, being heckled by other diners. Sheehy once had been a smooth, self-possessed character whose authority was beyond question. "If you saw the guy now," says my stockbroker friend, "you'd buy him a cup o' tea."

The Irish real estate bubble was different from the American version in many ways. It wasn't disguised, for a start. It didn't require a lot of complicated financial engineering beyond the

---

* On July 10, 2011, after a phone-hacking scandal, *News of the World* was closed.

understanding of mere mortals. It also wasn't as cynical. There aren't a lot Irish financiers, or real estate people, who have emerged with a future. In America the banks went down but the big shots in them still got rich; in Ireland the big shots went down with the banks. Sean Fitzpatrick, a working-class kid turned banker who built Anglo Irish Bank more or less from scratch, is widely viewed as the chief architect of Ireland's misfortune: today he is not merely bankrupt but unable to show his face in public. Mention his name and people with no interest in banking will tell you with disgust how he disguised millions of euros of loans made to himself by his own bank. What they don't mention is what he did with the money: invested it in Anglo Irish bonds! When the bank failed Fitzpatrick was listed among its creditors, having (in April 2008!) purchased five million euros of Anglo Irish subordinated floating rate notes.

The top executives of all three big banks operated in a similar spirit: they bought shares in their own companies right up to the moment of collapse, and continued to pay dividends, as if they had capital to burn. Virtually all of the big Irish property developers who behaved recklessly signed personal guarantees for their loans. It's widely assumed that they must be hiding big piles of money somewhere, but the evidence thus far suggests that they are not. The Irish Property Council has counted twenty-nine suicides by property developers since the crash—in a country where suicide often goes unreported and undercounted. "I said to all the guys, 'Always take money off the table.' Not many of them took money off the table," says Dermont Desmond, an Irish billionaire who made his fortune from software in the early 1990s, and so counts as old money.

The Irish nouveau riche may have created a Ponzi scheme, but it was a Ponzi scheme in which they themselves believed. So, too, for that matter, did some large number of ordinary Irish citizens who bought houses for fantastic sums. Ireland's 87 percent rate of homeownership is the highest in the world. There's no such thing as a nonrecourse mortgage in Ireland: the guy who pays too much for his house is not allowed simply to hand the keys to the bank and walk away. He's on the hook, personally, for whatever he borrowed. Across Ireland people are unable to extract themselves from their houses or their bank loans. Irish people will tell you that, because of their sad history of dispossession, owning a home is not just a way to avoid paying rent but a mark of freedom. In their rush to freedom, the Irish built their own prisons. And their leaders helped them to do it.

JUST BEFORE THE closing bell, the two men who sold the Irish people on the notion that they were responsible not merely for their own disastrous financial decisions but also for the ones made by their banks arrive in the chamber: Prime Minister Brian Cowen and Finance Minister Brian Lenihan. Along with the leader of the opposition, and the third in command of their own party, both are children of politicians who died in office: Irish politics is a family affair. Cowen happens also to have been the minister of finance from 2004 until mid-2008, when most of the bad stuff happened. He is not an obvious Leader of Men. His movements are sullen and lumbering, his face numbed by corpulence, his natural resting expression a look of confusion. One morning a few weeks before, he went on national radio sounding, to well-trained Irish ears, drunk. To my less trained ones he sounded merely groggy, but the public is in no mood to cut him a break. (Four different Irish people told me, on great authority, that Cowen had faxed Ireland's 440-billion-euro bank guarantee into the European Central Bank from a pub.) And the truth is, if you were to design a human being to maximize the likelihood that people would assume he drank too much you'd have a hard time doing better than the Irish prime minister. Brian Lenihan, who follows on Cowen's bovine heels, comes across, by comparison, as a decathlete in peak condition.

On this day, incredibly yet predictably, the Parliament decides not to hold a vote to fill three of its four empty seats. Then they adjourn, and I spend an hour with Joan Burton. Of the major parties in Ireland, Labor offers the closest thing to a dissenting opinion and a critique of Irish capitalism. As one of only eighteen members of the Irish House of Commons who voted against guaranteeing the banks' debts, Burton retains rare credibility. And in an hour of chatting about this and that she strikes me as straight, bright, and basically good news. But her role in the Irish drama is as clear as Morgan Kelly's: she's the shrill mother no one listened to. She speaks in exclamation points with a whiny voice that gets on the nerves of every Irishman—to the point where her voice is parodied on national radio. Now, when I ask her what she would do differently from what the Irish government is doing, even she is stumped. Like every other Irish politician, she is at the mercy of forces beyond her control. The Irish bank debt is now Irish government debt, and any suggestion of default will only raise the cost of borrowing the foreign money they now can't live without. "Do you know that Irish people are now experts on bonds?" says Burton. "Yes, they now say one hundred basis points rather than one percent! They have developed a new vocabulary!"

As the scope of the Irish losses has grown clearer, private investors have been less and less willing to leave even overnight deposits in Irish banks, and completely uninterested in buying longer-term bank bonds. The European Central Bank has quietly filled the void: one of the most closely watched numbers in Europe has been the amount the ECB has loaned to the big Irish banks. In late 2007, with the markets still suspending their disbelief, the banks had borrowed 6.5 billion euros. By December of 2008 the number had jumped to 45 billion. As Burton spoke to me the number was rising, from around 86 billion to a fresh high of 97 billion. That is, from November 2007 to October 2010 the Irish banks have borrowed 97 billion euros from the European Central Bank to repay private creditors. In September 2010 the last big chunk of money the Irish banks owed to their bondholders, 26 billion euros, came due. Once the bondholders were paid off in full, a window of opportunity for the Irish government closed. A default of the banks would now not be a default to private investors but a bill presented directly to European governments. This, by the way, is why there are so many important-looking foreigners in Dublin dining alone at night. They're here to make sure someone gets his money back.

One measure of how completely the Irish can't imagine offending their foreign financial rulers is how quickly Burton declines to contemplate such a default. She bears no responsibility at all for the banks' private debts, and yet when we creep up on the possibility of simply walking away from them, she veers away. Actually, she ups and leaves. "Oh, I have to go," she says. "I have to meet the finance minister with the bad news." Lenihan has called a private meeting with the opposition so that its leaders will be the first to hear of the draconian new Irish budget. This meeting is held not inside the Parliament, where the media can be kept at arm's length, but in a nearby building where the media are allowed to congregate. "We tried to have it in here but he moved it outside," says Burton. "He's taken to bringing us in to tell us the bad news first, so that when we walk out we're the ones announcing it to the media." She smiles. "He's tricky that way."

**BRIAN LENIHAN IS** the last remaining Irish politician anywhere near power whose mere appearance does not cause people on the streets of Dublin to explode with either scorn or laughter. He came to the job just weeks before the crisis, and so escapes blame for its origins. He's a barrister, not a financial or real estate person, with a proven ability to earn a good living without being bribed by property developers. He comes from a family of political people who are thought to have served honorably, or at any rate not used politics to enrich themselves. And, in December 2009, he was diagnosed with pancreatic cancer. Anyone who has been anywhere near an Irish

Catholic family knows that the member who has had the most recent run of bad luck enjoys exalted status—the right to do pretty much whatever he wants to do while everyone else squirms in silence. Since news of Lenihan's illness broke— just days after he'd learned of it himself, apparently, and before he'd told his children— he's minimized his suffering. Running under the public opinion polls that show the Irish feel a lot better about the minister of finance than they do about other politicians in his party is a common, unspoken understanding of his bravery.*

Brian Lenihan is also, as Joan Burton pointed out, tricky. It's racing up on eight in the evening when I meet him in a Department of Finance conference room. He's spent most of his day defending the harshest spending cuts and tax hikes in Irish history to Irish politicians, without offering any details about who, exactly, will pay for the bank's losses. (He's waiting until after the single by-election that the Dáil authorized is held.) He smiles. "Why is everyone so interested in Ireland?" he asks, almost innocently. "There's really far too much interest in us right now."

"Because you're interesting?" I say.

"Oh no," he's says, seriously. "We're not, really."

---

* Lenihan died in June 2011, seven months after this interview.

He proceeds to make the collapse of the Irish economy as uninteresting as possible. This awkward social responsibility—normalizing a freak show—is now a meaningful part of the job of being Ireland's finance minister. At just the moment the crazy uncle leapt from the cellar, the drunken aunt lurched through the front door—and, in front of the entire family and many important guests, they carved each other to bits with hunting knives. Daddy must now reassure eyewitnesses that they didn't see what they think they saw.

But the evidence that something deeply weird just happened in Ireland is still too conspicuous. A mile from the conference table where we take our seats you can still find a moonscape of vast two-year-old craters from which office parks were once meant to rise. Fully finished skyscrapers sit empty, water pooling on their lobby floors. There's a skeleton of a tower, cranes at rest on either side, like parentheses. It was meant to house Anglo Irish Bank. There's an empty new conference center that cost 75 million euros to build that has never been hooked up to the Dublin sewer and water systems. There's a city dump for which a developer paid 412 million euros in 2006—and which is now, when you include the cleanup costs, valued at *negative* 30 million euros. "Ireland is very unusual," says William Newsom, who has forty years of experience valuing commercial real estate for Savills in London. "There are whole swaths of either undeveloped land with planning permission or even partially developed sites which for practical purposes have zero value." The peak of the Irish madness is frozen in time for all to see. There's even an empty Starbucks, in the heart of what was meant to be a global financial center to rival London, where a carton of low-fat milk curdles beside a silver barista pitcher. The finance minister might as well be standing in front of Pompeii and saying that the volcano wasn't really worth mentioning. *Just a little lava!*

"THIS ISN'T ICELAND," is what he actually says. "We're not a hedge fund that's populated by 300,000 farmers and fishermen. Ireland is not going back to the eighties or the nineties. This is all in a much narrower band." And then he goes off on a soliloquy, the main point of which is: Ireland's problems are solvable and I am in control of the situation.

Back in September 2008, however, there was evidence that he wasn't. On September 17 the financial markets were in turmoil. Lehman Brothers had failed two days earlier, and the shares of Irish banks were plummeting and big corporations were withdrawing their deposits from them. Late that night Lenihan phoned David

McWilliams, a former research analyst with UBS in Zurich and London, who had moved back home to Dublin and turned himself into a writer and media personality. McWilliams had been loudly skeptical about the Irish real estate boom. Two weeks earlier he'd appeared on a television show with Lenihan: Lenihan had seemed to him entirely untroubled by the turmoil in the financial markets. Now he wanted to drive out and ask McWilliams's advice on what to do about the Irish banks.

The peculiar scene appears in McWilliams's charmingly indiscreet book *Follow the Money*. Lenihan arrives at the McWilliams residence, a forty-five minute drive outside of Dublin, marches through to the family kitchen, and pulls a hunk of raw garlic out of his jacket pocket. "He kicked off by saying if his officials knew he was here in my house, there'd be war," writes McWilliams. The finance minister stayed until two in the morning, peeling cloves of raw garlic and eating them, and anxiously picking McWilliams's brain. McWilliams came away with the feeling that the minister didn't entirely trust the advice he was getting from the people around him—and that he was not merely worried but confused. McWilliams told me that he sensed the mental state of the Finance Ministry was "complete chaos."

A week later the Irish Finance Ministry hired

investment bankers from Merrill Lynch to advise them. Some might say that if you were asking Merrill Lynch for financial advice in 2008 you were already in trouble, but that is not entirely fair. The bank analyst who had been most prescient and interesting about the Irish banks worked for Merrill Lynch. His name was Philip Ingram. In his late twenties, and a bit quirky—at Cambridge University he'd prepared for a career in zoology—Ingram had done something original and useful. He'd shined a new light on the way Irish banks lent against commercial real estate.

The commercial real estate loan market is generally less transparent than the market for home loans. The deals between bankers and property developers are one-off, on terms unknown to all but a few insiders. The parties to any loan always claim it is prudent: a bank analyst has little choice but to take them at their word. But Ingram was skeptical of the Irish banks. He had read Morgan Kelly's newspaper articles and even paid Kelly a visit in his University College office. To Ingram's eyes there appeared to be a vast difference between what the Irish banks were saying and what they were doing. To get at it he ignored what they were saying and went looking for knowledgeable insiders in the commercial property market. He interviewed them, as a journalist might. On

March 13, 2008, six months before the Irish real estate Ponzi scheme collapsed, Ingram published a report in which he simply quoted verbatim what market insiders had told him about various banks' lending to commercial real estate developers. The Irish banks were making far riskier loans in Ireland than they were in Britain, but even in Britain, the report revealed, they were the nuttiest lenders around: in that category, Anglo Irish, Bank of Ireland, and AIB came, in that order, first, second, and third.

FOR A FEW hours the Merrill Lynch report was the hottest read in the London financial markets, until Merrill Lynch retracted it. Merrill was the lead underwriter of Anglo Irish's bonds and the corporate broker to AIB: they'd earned huge sums of money off the growth of Irish banking. Moments after Phil Ingram hit the Send button on his report, the banks called their Merrill Lynch bankers and threatened to take their business elsewhere. The same executive from Anglo Irish Bank who had called to scream at Morgan Kelly called a Merrill research analyst to scream some more. ("I thought your work was fucking shit!") Ingram's superiors at Merrill Lynch hauled him into meetings with in-house lawyers who rewrote his report, purging it of its pointed language and its damning quotes from market insiders, including their many references to Irish banks.

Ingram's immediate boss in the research department, a fellow named Ed Allchin, was made to apologize to Merrill's investment bankers individually for the trouble he'd caused them. And from that moment everything Ingram wrote about Irish banks was rewritten and bowdlerized by Merrill Lynch's lawyers. At the end of 2008 Merrill fired him.

It would have been difficult for Merrill Lynch's investment bankers not to know, on some level, that, in a reckless market, the Irish banks acted with a recklessness all their own. But in the six-page memo to Brian Lenihan—for which the Irish taxpayer forked over to Merrill Lynch 7 million euros—they kept whatever reservations they might have had to themselves. "All of the Irish banks are profitable and well-capitalized," wrote the Merrill Lynch advisers, and then went on to suggest that their problem wasn't at all the bad loans they had made but the panic in the market. The Merrill Lynch memo listed a number of possible responses the Irish government might have to any run on Irish banks. It refrained from explicitly recommending one course of action over another, but its analysis of the problem implied that the most sensible thing to do was to guarantee the banks. After all, the banks were "fundamentally sound." Promise to eat all losses, and markets would quickly settle down—and the Irish banks would go back to being in perfectly good shape. As there would be no losses, the promise would be free.

What exactly was said in the meeting on the night of September 29, 2008, remains, amazingly, something of a secret. The government has refused Freedom of Information Act requests for the notes taken by participants. Apart from the prime minister and the bank regulators, the only people at the conference table inside the Ministry of Finance were the heads of the two yet-to-be disgraced big Irish banks: AIB and Bank of Ireland. Evidently they either lied to Brian Lenihan about the extent of their losses or didn't know themselves what those were. Or both. "At the time they were all saying the same thing," an Irish bank analyst tells me. " 'We don't have any subprime.' " What they meant was that they had avoided lending to American subprime borrowers; what they neglected to mention was that, in the general frenzy, all of Ireland had become subprime. Otherwise sound Irish borrowers had been rendered unsound by the size of the loans they had taken out to buy inflated Irish property. That had been the strangest consequence of the Irish bubble: to throw a nation that had finally clawed its way out of centuries of indentured servitude back into indentured servitude.

The report from Merrill Lynch asserting that the banks were "fundamentally sound" buttressed whatever story the banks told the finance minister. The Irish government's bank regulator, Patrick Neary, had echoed Merrill's judgment. Morgan Kelly was still a zany egghead; at any rate, no one who took him seriously was present in the room. Anglo Irish's stock had fallen 46 percent that day; AIB's had fallen 15 percent; there was a fair chance that when the stock exchange reopened one or both of them would go out of business. In the general panic, absent government intervention, the other banks would have gone down with Anglo Irish. Lenihan faced a choice: Should he believe the people immediately around him or the financial markets? Should he trust the family or the experts? He stuck with the family. Ireland gave its promise. And the promise sank Ireland.

EVEN AT THE time, the decision seemed a bit odd. The Irish banks, like the big American banks, managed to persuade a lot of people that they were so intertwined with their economy that their failure would bring down a lot of other things, too. But they weren't, at least not all of them. Anglo Irish Bank had only six branches, no ATMs, and no organic relationship with Irish business except the property developers. It lent money to people to buy land and build: that's all it did. It did this with money it had borrowed from foreigners. It was not, by nature, systemic.

It became so only when its losses were made everyone's.

In any case, if the Irish wanted to save their banks, why not guarantee just the deposits? There's a big difference between depositors and bondholders: depositors can flee. The immediate danger to the banks was that savers who had put money into them would take their money out, and the banks would be without funds. The investors who owned the roughly 80 billion euros' worth of Irish bank bonds, on the other hand, were stuck. They couldn't take their money out of the bank. And their 80 billion euros very nearly exactly covered the eventual losses inside the Irish banks. These private bondholders didn't have any right to be made whole by the Irish government. The bondholders didn't even *expect* to be made whole by the Irish government. Not long ago I spoke with a former senior Merrill Lynch bond trader who, on September 29, 2008, owned a pile of bonds in one of the Irish banks. He'd already tried to sell them back to the bank for 50 cents on the dollar—that is, he'd offered to take a huge loss, just to get out of them. On the morning of September 30 he awakened to find his bonds worth 100 cents on the dollar. The Irish government had guaranteed them! He couldn't believe his luck.

Across the financial markets this episode repeated itself. People who had made a private bet that had gone wrong and didn't expect to be repaid in full were handed their money back—from the Irish taxpayer.

In retrospect, now that the Irish bank losses are known to be world historically huge, the decision to cover them appears not merely odd but suicidal. A handful of Irish bankers incurred debts they could never repay, of something like 100 billion euros. They may have had no idea what they were doing, but they did it all the same. Their debts were private—owed by them to investors around the world—and still the Irish people have undertaken to repay them as if they were obligations of the state. For two years they have labored under this impossible burden with scarcely a peep of protest. What's more, all of the policy decisions since September 29, 2008, have set the hook more firmly inside the mouths of the Irish public. In January 2009 the Irish government nationalized Anglo Irish and its losses of 34 billion euros (and mounting). In late 2009 they created the National Asset Management Agency, the Irish version of the Troubled Asset Relief Program (TARP), but, unlike the U.S. government, actually followed through, and bought 80 billion euros' worth of crappy assets from the Irish banks.

A SINGLE DECISION sank Ireland, but when I ask Lenihan about it he becomes impatient, as if it isn't a fit topic for conversation. It wasn't much of a decision, he says, as he had no choice. Irish financial market rules are patterned on English law, and under English law the bondholders enjoy the same status as the ordinary depositors. That is, it was against the law to protect the little people with deposits in the bank without also saving the big investors who owned Irish bank bonds.

This rings a bell. When U.S. Treasury Secretary Hank Paulson realized that allowing Lehman Brothers to fail was viewed not as brave and principled but catastrophic, he, too, claimed he'd done what he'd done because the law gave him no other option. In the heat of the crisis, Paulson neglected to mention the law, just as Lenihan didn't bring up the law requiring him to pay off the banks' private lenders until long after he'd done it. In both cases the explanation was legalistic: narrowly true, but generally false. The Irish government always had the power to impose losses on even the senior bondholders, if it wanted to. "Senior people have forgotten that the government has certain powers," as Morgan Kelly puts it. "You can conscript people. You can send them off to certain death. *You can change the law*."

On September 30, 2008, in the heat of the moment, Lenihan gave the same argument for guaranteeing the bank's debts as Merrill Lynch:

to prevent "contagion." Tell financial markets that a loan to an Irish bank was a loan to the Irish government and investors would calm down. For who would doubt the credit of the Irish government? A few months later, when suspicions arose that the bank losses were so vast that they might bankrupt the Irish government, Lenihan offered a new reason for the government's gift to private investors: the bonds were owned by Irish savings banks. Up until then the government's line had been that they did not have any idea who owned the bank's bonds. Now they said that if the Irish government didn't eat the losses, Irish savers would pay the price. The Irish, in other words, were simply saving the Irish. This wasn't true: it provoked a cry of outrage from the Irish savings banks, who said they didn't own the bonds, and that they disapproved of the government's bestowing a huge gift on those who did. A political investigative blog called *Guido Fawkes* somehow obtained a list of the foreign bondholders: German banks, French banks, German investment funds, Goldman Sachs. (Yes: even the Irish did their bit for Goldman.)

ACROSS EUROPE JUST now men who thought their title was "minister of finance" have woken up to the idea that their job is actually government bond salesman. The Irish bank losses have obviously bankrupted Ireland, but the Irish finance minister does not want to talk about that. Instead he mentions to me, several times, that Ireland is "fully funded" until next summer. That is, the Irish government has enough cash in the bank to pay its bills until next July.

It isn't until I'm on my way out the door that I realize how trivial this point is. The blunt truth is that since September 2008 Ireland has been every day more at the mercy of her creditors. To remain afloat, Ireland's banks, which are now owned by the Irish government, have taken short-term loans from the European Central Bank of 85 billion euros. Inside of a week Lenihan will be compelled by the European Union to invite the IMF into Ireland, relinquish control of Irish finances, and accept a bailout package. The Irish public doesn't yet know it, but, even as the minister of finance and I sit together at his conference table, the European Central Bank has lost interest in lending to Irish banks. And soon Brian Lenihan will stand up in the Irish parliament and offer a fourth explanation for why private investors in Ireland's banks cannot be allowed to take losses. "There is simply no way that this country, whose banks are so dependent on international investors, can unilaterally renege on senior bondholders against the wishes of the ECB," he will say.

But there was once a time when the wishes of

the ECB didn't matter so much to Ireland. That time was before the Irish government used ECB money to pay off the foreign bondholders in Irish banks.

ONCE A DECADE I experiment with driving on the wrong side of the road, and wind up destroying dozens of side-view mirrors on cars parked on the left. When I went looking for some Irish person to drive me around, the result was a fellow I will call Ian McRory, who is Irish, and a driver, but pretty clearly a lot of other things, too. He has what appears to be a military-grade navigational system, for instance, and surprising knowledge about abstruse and secretive matters. "I do some personal security, and things of that nature," he says, when I ask him what else he does other than drive financial-disaster tourists back and forth across Ireland, and leaves it at that. Later, when I mention the name of a formerly rich Irish property developer, he says, casually, as if it were all in a day's work, that he had "let himself into" the fellow's vacation house and snapped photographs of the interior "for a man I know who is thinking of buying it."

Ian turns out to have a good feel for what little I, or anyone else, might find interesting in rural Ireland. He will say, for example, "Over there, that's a pretty typical fairy ring," and then explain, interestingly, that these circles of stones or mushrooms that occur seemingly naturally in Irish fields are believed by local farmers to house mythical creatures. "Irish people actually believe in fairies?" I will ask, straining but failing to catch a glimpse of the typical fairy ring to which Ian has just pointed. "I mean if you walked right up and asked him to his face, 'Do you believe in fairies?' most guys will deny it," he will reply. "But if you ask him to dig out the fairy ring on his property, he won't do it. To my way of thinking that's believing." And it is. It's a tactical belief, a belief that exists because the upside to disbelief is too small, like the former Irish belief that Irish land prices could rise forever.

The highway out of Dublin runs past abandoned building sites and neighborhoods without people in them. "We can stop at ghost estates on the way," says Ian, as we clear the suburbs of Dublin. "But if we stop at every one of them, we'll never get out of here." We pass wet green fields carved by potato farmers into small plots and, every now and then, a small village, but even the inhabited places feel desolate. The Irish countryside remains a place people flee. Among its drawbacks, from the outsider's point of view, is the weather. "It's always either raining or about to rain," says Ian. "I drove a black guy from Africa around the country once. It's raining the whole time. He says to me, 'I don't know why people live here. It's like living under an elephant.'"

The wet hedgerows cultivated along the highway to hide the wet road from the wet houses now hide the wet houses from the wet road. PICTURE OF THE VILLAGE OF THE FUTURE, reads a dripping billboard with a picture of a village that will never be built. Randomly selecting a village that appears to be more or less finished, we pull off the road. It's an exurb, without a suburb. GLEANN RIADA, reads the self-important sign in front. It's a few dozen houses in a field, attached to nothing but each other, ending with unoccupied slabs of concrete buried in weeds. You can see the moment the money stopped flowing from the Irish banks, the developer folded his tent, and the Polish workers went home. "The guys who laid this didn't even believe it was supposed to be finished," says Ian. The concrete slab, like the completed houses, is riven by the cracks that you see in a house after a major earthquake but which in this case are caused by carelessness. Inside, the floors are littered with trash and debris, the fixtures have been ripped out of the kitchen, and mold spreads spiderlike across the walls. The last time I saw an interior like this was in New Orleans after Katrina.

Ireland's Department of the Environment published its first audit of the country's new housing stock in 2009, after inspecting 2,846 housing developments, many of them ghost estates. The government granted planning permission for 180,000 units, of which more than 100,000 are unoccupied. Some of those that are occupied remain unfinished. Virtually all construction has now ceased. There aren't enough people in Ireland to fill the new houses; there were never enough people in Ireland to fill the new houses. Ask Irish property developers who they imagined was going to live in the Irish countryside and they all laugh the same uneasy laugh and offer up the same list of prospects: Poles; foreigners looking for second homes; entire departments of Irish government workers, who would be shipped to the sticks in a massive, planned relocation plan that somehow never materialized; the diaspora of seventy million human beings with some genetic link to Ireland. The problem that no one paid all that much attention to during the boom was that people from outside Ireland, even those with a genetic link to the place, have no interest in owning houses in Ireland. "This isn't an international property market," says an agent at Savills's Dublin branch named Ronan O'Driscoll. "There aren't any foreign buyers. There were never foreign buyers." Dublin was never London. The Irish countryside will never be the Cotswolds.

WHICH WAY ENTIRE nations jumped when the money was made freely available to them obviously told you a lot about them: their desires, their constraints, their secret sense of themselves. How they reacted when the money was taken away was equally revealing. In Greece the money was borrowed by the state: the debts are the debts of the Greek people, but the people want no part of them. The Greeks already have taken to the streets, violently, and have been quick to find people outside of Greece to blame for their problems: monks, Turks, foreign bankers. Greek anarchists now mail bombs to German politicians and hurl Molotov cocktails at their own police. In Ireland the money was borrowed by a few banks, and yet the people seem not only willing to repay it but to do so without so much as a small moan. Back in the autumn of 2008, after the government threatened to means-test the medical care, the old people had marched in the streets of Dublin. A few days after I'd arrived, the students followed suit, but their protest was less public anger than theater, and perhaps an excuse to skip school. (DOWN WITH THIS SORT OF THING, read one of the signs.) I'd tapped two students as they stumbled away from the event, to ask them why they had all painted yellow streaks onto their faces. They looked at each other for a beat. "Dunno!" one finally said, and burst out laughing.

Other than that . . . silence. It's more than three years since the Irish government foisted the losses of the Irish banks on the Irish people, and in that time there have been only two conspicuous acts of Irish social unrest. In early 2009, at AIB's first shareholder meeting after the collapse, a senior citizen hurled rotten eggs at the bank's executives. And late one night in September 2010, a property developer from Galway named Joe McNamara painted his cement mixer with anti-banker slogans, climbed inside the cab, drove across the country, and, after locking its brakes and disabling the release, stalled the machine between the gates of the Parliament. The elderly egg-thrower was a distant memory, but McNamara was still, more or less, in the news: declining requests for interviews. "Joe is a private person," his lawyer told me. "Joe feels like he's made his point. He doesn't want any media attention."

Before he'd parked his cement mixer in the Parliament's driveway, McNamara had been a small-time builder. He'd started out laying foundations, and, like a lot of tradesmen from the sticks, he'd been given a loan by Anglo Irish Bank. Thus began his career as a property developer. He'd moved to Galway, into a tacky new development beside a golf course, but the source of his financial distress lay an hour or so beyond the city, in a resort hotel he'd tried to build in the tiny village in which he'd grown up, called Keel, on a remote island called Achill.

"Achill," says Ian, after I tell him that's where I'd like him to drive me, then goes silent for a minute, as if giving me time to reconsider. "This time of year Achill's going to be fairly bleak." He thinks another minute. "Mind you, in the summer it can be fairly bleak as well."

It's twilight as we roll across the tiny bridge and onto the island. On either side of the snaking single-lane road, peat bogs stretch as far as the eye can see. The feel is less "tourist destination" than "end of the earth." ("The next stop is Newfoundland," says Ian.) The Achill Head Hotel—Joe's first venture, still run by his ex-wife—was closed and dark. But there, smack in the middle of the tiny village of his hometown of Keel, was the source of all of Joe McNamara's financial troubles: a giant black hole, surrounded by bulldozers and materials. He'd set out in 2005 to build a modest one-story hotel with twelve rooms. In April 2006, with the Irish property market exploding, he'd expanded his ambition and applied for permission to build a multistory luxury hotel. At exactly that moment, the market turned. "We went away in June of 2006," Ronan O'Driscoll, the Savills broker, told me. "We came back in September and everything had just stopped. How does everyone decide at once that it is time to stop—that it's become mad?"

For the past four years the hotel site had scarred the village. But it wasn't until May 2010 that

Anglo Irish Bank, which had lent McNamara the money to develop it, threatened to force him into receivership. Irish bankruptcy laws were not designed for spectacular failure, perhaps because the people who wrote them never imagined spectacular success. When a bank forces an Irish person into receivership, it follows up with a letter to his blood relations, informing them of his insolvency—and his shame. A notice of the bankruptcy is published in one national and one local newspaper. For as many as twelve years the Irish bankrupt is not permitted to take out a loan for more than 650 euros, or to own assets amounting to more than 3,100 euros, or to travel abroad without government permission. For twelve years part of what he earns may pass directly to his creditors. "It's not like the United States, where being bankrupt is almost a badge of honor," says Patrick White, of the Irish Property Council. "Here you are effectively disbarred from commercial life."

There is an ancient rule of financial life—if you owe the bank 5 million bucks, the bank owns you, but if you owe the bank 5 billion bucks, you own the bank—that newly applies to Ireland. The debts of Ireland's big property developers—defined as anyone who owed the bank more than 20 million euros—are now being worked out behind closed doors. In exchange for helping the government to manage or liquidate their real estate portfolios, the biggest failures have been spared bankruptcy. Smaller developers, like McNamara, are in a far harder place; and while no one seems to know how many of these people exist, the number is clearly big. Ireland's National Asset Management Agency controls roughly 80 billion euros' worth of commercial property loans. An Irish property expert named Peter Bacon, who advised NAMA when it was created, recently revealed that when he'd added up the smaller Irish property-related loans (those under 20 million euros), they amounted to another 80 billion euros. Some very large number of former Irish tradesmen are in exactly Joe McNamara's situation. Some very large number of Irish *homeowners* are in something very like it.

The difference between McNamara and everyone else is that he'd complained about it, publicly. But then, apparently, had genuinely thought better of it. I'd tracked down and phoned his ex-wife, who just laughed and told me to get lost. I finally reached McNamara himself, ambushing him on his cell phone. But he only muttered something about not wanting to draw further attention to himself, then hung up. It was only after I texted him to say I was en route to his hometown that he became sufficiently aroused to communicate. "What are you doing in Keel????" he hollered by text message, more than once. "Tell me *Why are you going to Keel???*" Then, once again, he fell silent. "The problem with the Irish people," Ian says, as we drive away from the black hole that bankrupted Joe McNamara, "is that you can push them and push them and push them. But when they break they go wacko." (A month later, after a period of silence, McNamara would reappear, screaming from the top of a building crane that he had driven across the country and ditched, once again, in front of the Parliament.)

TWO THINGS STRIKE every Irish person when he comes to America, Irish friends tell me: the vastness of the country, and the seemingly endless desire of its people to talk about their personal problems. Two things strike an American when he comes to Ireland: how small it is, and how tight-lipped. An Irish person with a personal problem takes it into a hole with him, like a squirrel with a nut before winter. He tortures himself and sometimes his loved ones, too. What he doesn't do, if he has suffered some reversal, is vent about it to the outside world. The famous Irish gift of gab is a cover for all the things they aren't telling you.

So far as I could see, by November 10, 2010, the population of Irish people willing to make a stink about what has happened to them had been reduced to one: the egg-thrower. The next day we pull up outside his home, a modest old row house on the outskirts of Dublin. The cheery elderly gentleman who opens the door in a neat burgundy sweater and well-pressed slacks has, among his other qualities, fantastically good manners. He has the ability to seem pleased even when total strangers ring his doorbell, and to make them feel welcome. On the table in Gary Keogh's small and tidy dining room is a book, created by his grandchildren, dated May 2009. *Granddad's Eggcellent Adventure*, it is called.

In the months after Brian Lenihan's bank bailout, Keogh, for the first time in his life, began to pay attention to the behavior of the Irish bankers. His own shares in AIB, once thought to be as sound as cash or gold, were rapidly becoming worthless, but the bank's executives exhibited not the first hint of remorse or shame. AIB's chairman, Dermot Gleeson, and its CEO, Eugene Sheehy, troubled him the most. "The two of 'em stood up, time and again, and said, 'Our bank is one hundred percent sound,'" explains Keogh. "As if nothing at all was the matter!" He set out to learn more about these people in whom he had always placed blind trust. What he found—high pay, corporate boondoggles— outraged him further. "The chairman paid himself four hundred seventy-five thousand to chair twelve meetings!" he still shouts.

What Keogh learned remains both the most shocking and the most familiar aspect of the Irish catastrophe: how easily ancient financial institutions abandoned their traditions and principles. An upstart bank, Anglo Irish, had entered their market, and professed to have found a new and better way to be a banker. Anglo made incredibly quick decisions: an Irish property developer could walk into Anglo's office in the late afternoon with a new idea and walk out with hundreds of millions of euros the same night. Anglo was able to shovel money out its door so quickly because it had turned banking into a family affair: if they liked the man they didn't bother to evaluate his project.

Rather than point out the insanity of the approach, the two old Irish banks simply caved to it. An Irish businessman named Denis O'Brien sat on the board of the Bank of Ireland in 2005, when it was faced with the astonishing growth of Anglo Irish. (Anglo Irish was about to *double* in size in just two years.) "I remember the CEO coming in and saying, 'We're going to grow at 30 percent a year,'" O Brien told me. "I said how the fuck are you going to do that? Banking is a five-to-seven-percent-a-year growth business at best."

They did it by doing what Anglo Irish had done: writing checks to Irish property developers to buy Irish land at any price. AIB, which had paid its lending officers based on how many dollars they lent, opened a unit nicknamed ABA (Anybody but Anglo), dedicated to poaching Anglo's biggest property developer clients—the very people who would become the most spectacular busts in Irish history. In October 2008 the *Irish Times* published a list of the five biggest real estate deals from the past three years. Allied Irish lent the money for ten of the fifteen, Anglo Irish for just one. On Irish national radio the insolvent property developer Simon Kelly, who personally owes 200 million euros to various Irish banks and who belongs to a partnership that owes another 2 billion euros, confessed that the only time in his career a banker became upset with him was when he *repaid* a loan, to Anglo Irish—with money borrowed from Allied Irish. The former Anglo Irish executives I interviewed (off the record, as they are all in hiding) speak of their older, more respectable imitators with a kind of amazement. "Yes, we were out of control," they say, in so many words. "But those guys were *fucking nuts*."

Gary Keogh thought about how Ireland had changed from his youth, when the country was dirt poor. "I used to collect bottle caps," he says. "Now the health service doesn't even bother to take back crutches anymore? No! We're far too wealthy." Unlike most people he knew, Keogh had no debts. "I had nothing to lose," he says. "I didn't owe anyone any money. That's why I could do it!" He'd also just recovered from a serious illness, and felt a bit as if he was playing with house money. "I had just got a new kidney and I was very pleased with it," he says. "But I think it must have been Che Guevera's kidney." He describes his elaborate plot the way an assassin might describe the perfect hit. "I only had two rotten eggs," he says, "but by God they were rotten! Because I kept them six weeks in the garage!"

The AIB shareholders meeting of March 2009 was the first he'd ever attended. He was, he admits, a bit worried something might go wrong. Worried parking might be a problem, he took the bus; worried that his eggs might break, he designed a container to protect them; worried that he didn't even know what the room looked like, he left himself time to case the meeting hall. "I got to the front door early and had a little recce," as he puts it, "just to see what was going to happen." His egg container was too large to sneak inside, so he ditched it. "I had one egg in each jacket pocket," he says. Worried that his eggs might be too slippery to grip and throw, he'd wrapped each of them in a thin layer of cellophane. "I positioned myself four rows back and four seats in," he says. "Not too close but not too far." Then he waited for his moment.

It came immediately. Right after the executives took their places at the dais, a shareholder stood up, uninvited, to ask a question. Gleeson, AIB's chairman, barked, "Sit down!"

"He thought he was a dictator!" says Keogh,

who had heard enough. He rose to his feet and shouted, "I've listened to enough of your crap! You're a fucking bastard!" And then he began firing.

"He thought he had been shot," he says now with a little smile, "because the first egg hit the microphone and went *Pow!*" It splattered onto the shoulder pad of Gleeson's suit. The second egg missed the CEO but nailed the AIB sign behind him.

Then the security guards were on him. "I was told I would be arrested and charged, but I never was," he says. Of course he wasn't: this was, at bottom, a family dispute. The guards wanted to escort him out, but he actually left the place on his own and climbed aboard the next bus home. "The incident happened at ten past ten in the morning," he says. "I was home by ten to eleven. At ten past eleven the phone rang. And I was on the radio for an hour." Then, but briefly, all was madness. "The press descended on the house and they wouldn't get out," he says. It didn't really matter; he wasn't sticking around. He'd done exactly what he'd planned to do and saw no need to make a further fuss. He flew out of Dublin Airport at six the next morning for a long-planned Mediterranean cruise.

# IV

## THE SECRET LIVES OF GERMANS

By the time I arrived in Hamburg, in the summer of 2011, the fate of the financial universe seemed to turn on which way the German people jumped. Moody's was set to downgrade the Portuguese government's debt to junk bond status, and Standard & Poor's had hinted darkly that Italy might be next. Ireland was about to be downgraded to junk status, too, and there was a very real possibility that the newly elected local Spanish governments might seize the moment to announce that the former local Spanish governments had miscalculated, and owed foreigners a lot more money than they previously imagined. Then there was Greece. Of the 126 countries with rated debt, Greece now ranked 126th: the Greeks were officially regarded as the least likely people on the planet to repay their debts. As the Germans were not only the biggest creditor of the various deadbeat European nations but their only serious hope for future funding, it was left to the Germans to act as moral arbiter, to decide which financial behaviors would be tolerated and which would not. As a senior official at the Bundesbank put it to me, "If we say no, it's no. Nothing happens without Germany. This is where the losses come to live." Just a year ago, when German public figures called Greeks cheaters, or German magazines ran headlines like WHY DON'T YOU SELL YOUR ISLANDS, YOU BANKRUPT GREEKS?, ordinary Greeks took it as an outrageous insult. In June of 2011 the Greek government started selling islands, or at any rate created a fire-sale list of thousands of properties—golf courses, beaches, airports, farmlands, roads—that they hoped to auction in order to help repay their debts. It's safe to say that the idea of doing this had not come from the Greeks.

To no one but a German is Hamburg an obvious place to spend a vacation, but it happened to be a German holiday, and Hamburg was overrun by German tourists. When I asked the hotel concierge what there was to see in his city, he had to think for a few seconds before he said, "Most people just go to the Reeperbahn." The Reeperbahn is Hamburg's red-light district, the largest red-light district in the world, according to one guidebook, though you have to wonder how anyone figured that out. And the Reeperbahn, as it happens, was why I was there.

Perhaps because they have such a gift for creating difficulties with non-Germans, the Germans have been on the receiving end of many scholarly attempts to understand their collective behavior. In this vast and growing enterprise a small book with a funny title towers over many larger, more ponderous ones. Written in the early 1980s by a distinguished American anthropologist named Alan Dundes, *Life Is Like a Chicken Coop Ladder* set out to describe the German character through the stories that ordinary Germans liked to tell one another. Dundes specialized in folklore, and in German folklore, as he put it, "one finds an inordinate number of texts concerning Scheisse (shit), Dreck (dirt), Mist (manure), Arsch (ass). . . . Folksongs, folktales, proverbs, riddles, folk speech—all attest to the Germans' longstanding special interest in this area of human activity."

He proceeded to pile up a shockingly high stack of evidence to support his theory. There's a popular German folk character called *der Dukatenscheisser* (The Money Shitter), who is commonly depicted crapping coins from his rear end. The world's first museum devoted exclusively to toilets is in Munich. (A second has opened in New Delhi.) The German word for "shit" performs a vast number of bizarre linguistic duties—for instance, a common German term of endearment once was "my little shitbag." The first thing Gutenberg sought to publish, after the Bible, was a laxative timetable he called a "Purgation-Calendar." Then there is the astonishing number of anal German folk sayings. "As the fish lives in water, so does the shit stick to the asshole!," to select but one of the seemingly endless examples.

Dundes caused a bit of a stir, for an anthropologist, by tracking this single low national character trait into the most important moments in German history. The fiercely scatological Martin Luther ("I am like ripe shit and the world is a gigantic ass-hole," Luther once explained) had the idea that launched the Protestant Reformation while sitting on the john. Mozart's letters revealed a mind, as Dundes put it, whose "indulgence in fecal imagery may be virtually unmatched." Hitler's favorite word was *Scheisskerl* (shithead): he apparently used it to describe not only other people but himself as well. After the war Hitler's doctors told U.S. intelligence officers that their patient had devoted surprising energy to examining his own feces; and there was pretty strong evidence that one of his favorite things to do with women was to have them poop on him. Perhaps Hitler was so persuasive to Germans, Dundes suggested, because he shared their quintessential trait, a public abhorrence of filth that masked a private obsession. "The combination of clean and dirty: clean exterior–dirty interior, or clean form and dirty content—is very much a part of the German national character," he wrote.

Dundes confined himself mainly to the study of low German culture. (For those hoping to examine coprophilia in German high culture he recommended another book, by a pair of German scholars, called *The Call of Human Nature: The Role of Scatology in Modern German Literature*.) Still, it was hard to come away from his treatise without the strong sense that all Germans, high and low, were a bit different from you and me— a point he made in the introduction to the paperback version of his book. "The American wife of a German-born colleague confessed to me that she understood her husband much better after reading the book," he wrote. "Prior to that time, she had wrongly assumed that he must have some kind of peculiar psychological hang-up inasmuch as he insisted upon discussing at great length the state of his latest bowel movement."

The Hamburg red-light district had caught Dundes's eye because the locals made such a big deal of mud wrestling. Naked women fought in a ring of filth while the spectators wore plastic caps, a sort of head condom, to avoid being splattered. "Thus," wrote Dundes, "the audience can remain clean while enjoying dirt!" Germans longed to be near the shit, but not in it. This, as it turns out, is an excellent description of their role in the current financial crisis.

A WEEK EARLIER, in Berlin, I had gone to see Germany's deputy minister of finance, a forty-four-year-old career government official named

Jörg Asmussen. The Germans now are in possession of the only Finance Ministry in the big-time developed world whose leaders don't need to worry whether their economy will collapse the moment investors stop buying their bonds. As unemployment in Greece climbs to the highest on record (16.2 percent, at last count), it falls in Germany to twenty-year lows (6.9 percent). Germany appears to have experienced a financial crisis without economic consequences. They'd donned head condoms in the presence of their bankers, and avoided being splattered by their mud. As a result, for the past year or so the financial markets have been trying and failing to get a read on the German people: they can obviously afford to pay off the debts of their fellow Europeans, but will they actually do it? Are they now Europeans, or are they still Germans? Any utterance or gesture by any German official anywhere near this decision for the past eighteen months has been a market-moving headline, and there have been plenty of them, most of them echoing German public opinion, and expressing incomprehension and outrage that other people can behave so irresponsibly. Asmussen is one of the Germans now being obsessively watched. Along with his boss, Wolfgang Schäuble, he's one of two German officials present in every conversation between the German government and the deadbeats.

The Finance Ministry, built in the mid-1930s, is a monument to both the Nazis' ambition and their taste. A faceless butte, it is so big that if you circle it in the wrong direction it can take you twenty minutes to find the front door. I circle it in the wrong direction, then sweat and huff to make up for lost time, all the while wondering if provincial Nazis in from the sticks had the same experience, wandering outside these forbidding stone walls trying to figure out how to get in. At length I find a familiar-looking courtyard: the only difference between its appearance now and in famous old photographs is that Hitler is no longer marching in and out of the entryway, and the statue of the eagle perched atop the swastika has been removed. "It was built for Göring's Air Ministry," says the waiting Finance Ministry public relations man, who is, oddly enough, French. "You can tell from the cheerful architecture." He explains that the building is so big because Hermann Göring wanted to be able to land planes on its roof.

I have arrived about three minutes late, but the German deputy minister of finance runs a full five minutes later, which, I will learn, is viewed by Germans almost as a felony. He apologizes a great deal more than he needs to for the delay. He wears the slender framed spectacles of a German film director, and is extremely fit and bald, but by choice rather than circumstance. Extremely fit white men who shave their heads are making a statement, in my experience of them. "I don't need body fat and I don't need hair," they seem to be saying, while also implying that anyone who does is a wuss. The deputy finance minister even laughs just as all extremely fit men with shaved heads should laugh, if they want to remain in character. Instead of opening his mouth to allow the air to pass, he purses his lips and snorts the sound out through his nose. He may need laughter as much as other men, but he needs less air to laugh with. His desk is a template of self-discipline. Alive with implied activity—legal pads, Post-it notes, manila folders—every single object on it is perfectly aligned with all the others and with the edges of the desk. Every angle is precisely ninety degrees. But the most striking optional décor is a big white sign on the wall beside the desk. It's in German but translates easily back into the original English:

THE SECRET OF SUCCESS IS TO UNDERSTAND THE POINT OF VIEW OF OTHERS.

—Henry Ford

This surprises me. It's not at all what an extremely fit bald man should have as his mantra. It's *soft*. The deputy German finance minister further disturbs my wild assumptions about him by speaking clearly, even recklessly, about subjects most finance ministers assume it is their job to obscure. He offers up, without much prompting, that he has just finished reading the latest unpublished report by IMF investigators on the progress made by the Greek government in reforming itself. "They have not implemented the measures they have promised to implement," he says simply. "They are not making the agreed-upon reforms."

"The people at the IMF put it *that* clearly?" I ask.

He turns to page seven of the IMF report, where it recommends not giving the Greeks the next tranche of the money the government needs to avoid defaulting on its bonds. "They have a massive problem still with revenue collection. Not the tax law itself. It's the *collection* which needs to be overhauled."

The Greeks are still refusing to pay their taxes, in other words. But it is only one of many Greek sins. "Their labor market isn't changing as it needs to." I ask him for an example. "They had very clearly as a tradition a thirteenth or fourteenth monthly salary," he says instantly. "Due to developments in the last ten years, a similar [civil service] job in Germany pays fifty-five thousand euros. In Greece is it seventy thousand." To get around pay restraints in the calendar year, the Greek government simply paid employees for months that didn't exist. "They need to change the relationship of the people to the government," he continues. "It is not a task that can be done in three months." Changing the relationship between any people and its government, he added, was not a trivial matter. The Greeks needed to change their culture. He couldn't have put this more bluntly: if the Greeks and the Germans were to coexist in a currency union, the Greeks needed to change who they are.

This is unlikely to happen soon enough to matter. The Greeks not only have massive debts but are still running big deficits. Trapped by an artificially strong currency, they cannot turn these deficits into surpluses, even if they do everything outsiders want them to do. Their exports, priced in euros, remain expensive. The German government wants the Greeks to slash the size of their government, but that will also slow economic growth and reduce tax revenues. And so one of two things must happen. Either the Germans must agree to integrate Europe fiscally, so that Germany and Greece bear the same relationship to each other as, say, Indiana and Mississippi—the tax dollars of ordinary Germans would go into a common coffer and be used to pay for the lifestyle of ordinary Greeks—or the Greeks (and probably, eventually, every non-German) must introduce "structural reform," a euphemism for magically and radically transforming themselves into a people as efficient and productive as the Germans. The first solution is pleasant for Greeks but painful for Germans. The second solution is pleasant for Germans but painful, possibly even suicidal, for Greeks.

The only economically plausible scenario is that the Germans, with a bit of help from a rapidly shrinking population of solvent European countries, suck it up, work harder, and pay for everyone else. But what is economically plausible appears to be politically unacceptable. The German people all know at least one fact about the euro: that before they agreed to trade in their deutsche marks their leaders promised them, explicitly, they would never be required to bail out other countries. The rule was created with the founding of the European Central Bank and was violated in 2010. Public opinion turns more against the violation every day—so much so that Chancellor Angela Merkel, who has a reputation for reading the public mood, hasn't even bothered to try to go before the German people to persuade them that it might be in their interest to help the Greeks.

That is why Europe's money problems feel not just problematic but intractable. It's why Greeks are now mailing bombs to Merkel, and thugs in Berlin are hurling stones through the windows of the Greek consulate. And it's why European leaders have done nothing but delay the inevitable reckoning, by scrambling every few months to find cash to plug the ever growing holes in Greece, Ireland, and Portugal, and praying that bigger and more alarming holes in Spain, Italy, and even France do not reveal themselves.

Until now the European Central Bank, in Frankfurt, has been the main source of this cash. The ECB was designed to behave with the same discipline as the Bundesbank but has been redesigned by the financial crisis into something else. Already, it has bought, outright, something like $80 billion in Greek and Irish and Portuguese government bonds, and lent another $450 billion or so to various European governments and European banks, accepting virtually any collateral, including Greek government bonds. But the ECB has a rule—and the Germans think the rule very important—that they cannot accept as collateral bonds classified by the U.S. rating agencies as in default. Given that the ECB once had a rule against buying bonds outright in the open market, and another rule against government bailouts, it's a little odd that they have gotten so hung up on this technicality. But they have. If Greece defaults on its debt, the ECB not only will lose a pile on its holdings of Greek bonds but must return the bonds to the European banks, and the European banks must fork over $450 billion in cash. The ECB itself might face insolvency, which would mean turning for funds to its solvent member governments, led by Germany. (The senior official at the Bundesbank told me they have already thought about how to deal with the request. "We have thirty-four hundred tons of gold," he said. "We are the only country that has not sold its original allotment [from the late 1940s]. So we are covered to some extent.")

The bigger problem with a Greek default is that it might well force other European countries and their banks themselves into default. At the very least it would create panic and confusion in the market for both sovereign and bank debt, at a time when a lot of banks and at least two big European debt-ridden countries, Italy and Spain, cannot afford panic and confusion.

At the bottom of this unholy mess, from the point of view of the German Finance Ministry, is the unwillingness, or inability, of the Greeks to change their behavior. That was what the currency union always implied: entire peoples had to change their way of life. Conceived as a tool for integrating Germany with Europe, and preventing the Germans from dominating others, the euro had become the opposite. For better or worse, the Germans now control the financial fate of Europe. If the rest of Europe was to continue to enjoy the benefits of what was essentially a German currency they'd need to become more

German. And so, once again, all sorts of people who would rather not think about what it means to be "German" are compelled to do so.

Jörg Asmussen offers the first hint of an answer in his personal behavior. He was a type familiar in Germany but absolutely freakish in Greece or, for that matter, the United States: a keenly intelligent, highly ambitious civil servant who had no other ambition but to serve his country. His sparkling curriculum vitae was missing a line that would be found on the résumés of men in his position almost everywhere else in the world—the line where he leaves government service for Goldman Sachs to cash out. When I asked another prominent German civil servant why he hadn't taken time out of public service to make his fortune working for some bank, the way every American civil servant who is anywhere near finance seems to want to do, his expression changed to alarm. "But I could never do this," he said. "It would be illoyal!" Asmussen echoes this sentiment when I ask him why he hasn't bothered to get rich.

He then addresses the German question more directly. The curious thing about the eruption of cheap and indiscriminate lending of money between 2002 and 2008 was the different effects it had from country to country. Every developed country was subjected to more or less the same temptation, but no two countries responded in precisely the same way. Much of Europe had borrowed money cheaply to buy stuff it couldn't honestly afford. In effect, lots of non-Germans had used Germany's credit rating to indulge their material desires. The Germans were the exception. Given the chance to take something for nothing, the German people simply ignored the offer. "There was no credit boom in Germany," says Asmussen. "Real estate prices were completely flat. There was no borrowing for consumption. Because this behavior is totally unacceptable in Germany. This is what the German people are. This is deeply in German genes. It is perhaps a leftover of the collective memory of the Great Depression and the hyperinflation of the 1920s." The German government was equally prudent because, he went on, "there is a consensus among the different parties about this: if you're not adhering to fiscal responsibility you have no chance in elections, because the people are that way."

In the moment of temptation Germany became something like a mirror image to Iceland and Ireland and Greece—and the United States. Other countries used foreign money to fuel various forms of insanity. The Germans, through their bankers, used their own money to enable foreigners to behave insanely.

This is what makes the German case so peculiar. If they had been merely the only big, developed nation with decent financial morals, they would present one sort of picture, of simple rectitude. But they had done something far less common: during the boom German bankers had gone out of their way to get dirty. They lent money to American subprime borrowers, to Irish real estate barons, to Icelandic banking tycoons, to do things that no German ever would do. The German losses are still being toted up, but at last count they stand at $21 billion in the Icelandic banks, $100 billion in Irish banks, $60 billion in various U.S. subprime-backed bonds, and some yet to be determined amount in Greek bonds. The only financial disaster in the last decade German bankers appear to have missed was investing with Bernie Madoff (perhaps the only advantage to the German financial system of having no Jews). In their own country, however, these seemingly crazed bankers behaved with restraint. The German people did not allow them to behave otherwise. It was another case of clean on the outside, dirty on the inside. The German banks that wanted to get a little dirty needed to go abroad to do it.

About this the deputy finance minister has not that much to say, though he does wonder, idly, how a real estate crisis in Florida ends with massive financial losses in Germany. That such a thing has happened seems genuinely to puzzle him.

A GERMAN ECONOMIST named Henrik Enderlein, who teaches at the Hertie School of Governance in Berlin, has described the radical change that occurred in German banks beginning about 2003. In a paper in progress, Enderlein points out, "Many observers initially believed German banks would be relatively less exposed to the crisis. The contrary turned out to be the case. German banks ended up being among the most affected in continental Europe and this despite relatively favorable economic conditions." Everyone thought that German bankers were more conservative, and more isolated from the outside world, than, say, the French. And it wasn't true. "There had never been any innovation in German banking," says Enderlein. "You gave money to some company, and the company paid you back. They went [virtually overnight] from this to being American. And they weren't any good at it."

What Germans did with money between 2003 and 2008 would never have been possible within Germany, as there was no one to take the other side of the many deals they did that made no sense. They lost massive sums, in everything they touched, from U.S. subprime loans to Greek government bonds. Indeed, one view of the European debt crisis—the Greek street view—is that it is an elaborate attempt by the German government on behalf of its banks to get their money back without calling attention to what they are up to. The German government gives money to the European Union rescue fund so that it can give money to the Irish government so that the Irish government can give money to Irish banks, so the Irish banks can repay their loans to the German banks. "They are playing billiards," says Enderlein. "The easier way to do it would be to give German money to the German banks and let the Irish banks fail." Why they don't simply do this is a question worth trying to answer.

THE TWENTY-MINUTE WALK from the German Finance Ministry to the office of the chairman of Commerzbank, one of Germany's two giant private banks, is punctuated by officially sanctioned memories: the new Holocaust Memorial, two and a half times the acreage occupied by the U.S. Embassy; the new street beside it, called Hannah Arendt Street; the signs pointing to Berlin's new Jewish Museum; the park that contains the Berlin Zoo, where, after spending decades denying they had ever mistreated Jews, the authorities have newly installed, on the Antelope House, a plaque commemorating their Nazi-era expropriation of shares in the zoo owned by Jews. Along the way you also pass Hitler's bunker, but you'd never know it was there, as it has been paved over by a parking lot, and the small plaque that commemorates it is well hidden. The streets of Berlin can feel like an elaborate shrine. It's as if history stopped and assigned roles to people, and the Germans have been required to accept that they will always play the villain. On the other hand, it's easier to express contrition about just about everything the less personally responsible one feels. The guilt is being so loudly expressed precisely because it is no longer personal and searing. Hardly anyone still alive is responsible for what happened here: everyone is. But when everyone is guilty, no one is.

At any rate, if some Martian landed on the streets of Berlin knowing nothing of its history, he might wonder: who are these people called "the Jews," and how did they come to run this place? But there are no Jews in Germany, or not many. "The German people never see Jews," says Gary Smith, the director of the American Academy in Berlin. "Jews are unreal to them. When they think of Jews they think of victims." The further away the German people get from their victims, the more conspicuously they commemorate them. Of course no German in his right mind actually wants to sit around remembering the terrible crimes committed by his ancestors—and there are signs, including the memorials, that they are finding ways to move on. A good friend of mine, a Jew whose family was driven out of Germany in the 1930s, recently visited a German consulate in the United States to apply for a passport. He already held one European passport, but he worried that the European Union might one day fall apart, and he wanted access to Germany, just in case. The German official in charge—an Aryan out of central casting, wearing a *Sound of Music* vest—handed him a copy of a pamphlet titled *A Jew's Life in Modern Germany.*

"Would you mind if we take a picture?" he asked my friend, after processing his passport application.

"No problem," said my friend.

"Can we do it in front of the flag?" asked the official.

My friend stared at the German flag. "What's this for?" he asked.

"Our website," said the German official, then added that the government hoped to post the photo with a sign that read: *This man is the descendant of Holocaust survivors and he has decided to return to Germany.*

COMMERZBANK WAS THE first private bank that the German government had to rescue during the financial crisis, with an injection of $25 billion, but that's not why it had caught my attention. I'd been walking around Frankfurt one night with a German financier when I noticed the Commerzbank building on the skyline. There's a law in Germany prohibiting buildings higher than twenty stories, but Frankfurt allows exceptions. The Commerzbank Tower is fifty-three stories high and unusually shaped: it resembles a giant throne. The top of the building, the arms of the throne, are more decorative than useful. The interesting thing, said the German financier, who visited often, is the glass room at the top, from which one looks down over Frankfurt. It is a men's toilet. Commerzbank executives had taken him there to show him how, in full view of the world below, he could shit on Deutsche Bank.

The Commerzbank chairman, Klaus-Peter Müller, actually works in Berlin, inside another very German kind of place. His office is attached to the side of the Brandenburg Gate. The Berlin Wall once ran, roughly speaking, right through the middle of it. One side of his building was once a field of fire for East German border guards, the other a backdrop for Ronald Reagan's famous speech. ("Mr. Gorbachev, open this gate. Mr. Gorbachev, tear down this wall!") From looking at it you would never guess any of this. "After the wall came down we were offered the chance to buy it back," says Müller. "This building had been ours before the war. But the condition was that we had to put everything back *exactly* the way it was. It all had to be *hand-*

*fabricated.*" He points out the seemingly antique brass doorknobs and the seemingly antique windows. Across Germany, in the past twenty years or so, town centers completely destroyed by bombs in World War II have been restored, stone by stone. The German government has agreed to pay some huge sum of money to rebuild the Berliner Schloss, the old Royal Palace that was leveled in the 1950s by the East German authorities, so that it will look exactly as it does in prewar photographs. If the trend continues, it will one day appear as if nothing terrible had ever happened in Germany, when *everything* terrible happened in it. "Do not ask me what it cost," the bank chairman says, and laughs.

He then offers me the same survey of German banking that I will hear from half a dozen others. German banks are not, like American banks, mainly private enterprises. Most are either explicitly state-backed or small savings co-ops. Commerzbank, Dresdner Bank, and Deutsche Bank, all founded in the 1870s, are the only three big private German banks. In 2009 Commerzbank bought Dresdner. Both turned out to be loaded with toxic assets, and so the merged bank required a government bailout. "We are not a proprietary trading nation," says Müller, getting pretty quickly to the nub of Germany's banking problems. German banking was never meant to be a high-stakes affair. Banking, done in the proper German fashion, is less a free enterprise than a utility. "Why should you pay twenty million to a thirty-two-year-old trader?" Müller asks himself. "He uses the office space, the IT, the business card with a first-class name on it. If I take the business card away from that guy he would probably sell hot dogs." This man is the German equivalent of the head of Bank of America or Citigroup. And he is actively hostile to the idea that bankers should make huge sums of money.

In the bargain, he tells me why the current financial crisis has so unsettled the German banker's view of the financial universe. In the early 1970s, after he started at Commerzbank, the bank opened the first New York branch of any German bank, and he went to work in it. He mists up a bit when he tells stories about the Americans he did business with back then: in one story, an American investment banker who had inadvertently shut him out of a deal hunts him down and hands him an envelope with seventy-five grand in it, because he hadn't meant for the German bank to get stiffed. "You have to understand," he says emphatically, "this is where I get my view of Americans." In the past few years, he adds, that view had changed. I sense a feeling of loss.

"How much money did you lose in subprime?" I ask.

"I don't want to tell you," he says.

He laughs and then continues. "For forty years we didn't lose a penny on anything with a triple-A rating," he says. "We stopped building the portfolio in subprime in 2006. I had the idea that there was something wrong with your market. I did not have the idea that your market would completely collapse." He pauses. "It has told something to me. I was in the belief that the best supervised of all banking systems was in New York. To me the Fed and the SEC were second to none. I did not believe that there would be e-mail traffic between investment bankers saying that they were selling . . ." He pauses again, and decides he shouldn't say "shit." "Dirt," he says. "This is by far my biggest professional disappointment. I was in a much too positive way U.S.-biased. I had a set of beliefs about U.S. values."

The global financial system may exist to bring borrowers and lenders together, but, over the past few decades, it has become something else, too: a tool for maximizing the number of encounters between the strong and the weak, so that the one might exploit the other. Extremely smart traders inside Wall Street investment banks devise deeply unfair, diabolically complicated bets, and then send their sales forces out to scour the world for some idiot who will take the other side of those bets. During the boom years a wildly disproportionate number of those idiots were in Germany. As a reporter for Bloomberg News in Frankfurt named Aaron Kirchfeld put it to me, "You'd talk to a New York investment banker and they'd say, 'No one is going to buy this crap. Oh. Wait. The Landesbanks will!'" When Morgan Stanley designed extremely complicated credit default swaps so they were all but certain to fail, so that their own proprietary traders could bet against them, the buyer was German. When Goldman Sachs helped the New York hedge fund manager John Paulson design a bond to bet against—a bond that Paulson hoped would fail—the buyer on the other side was a German bank called IKB. IKB, along with another famous fool at the Wall Street poker table called WestLB, was based in Düsseldorf—which is why, when you asked a smart Wall Street subprime mortgage bond trader circa June 2007 who was still buying his crap, he could say, simply, "Stupid Germans in Düsseldorf."

**THE DRIVE FROM** Berlin to Düsseldorf takes longer than it should. For long stretches the highway is choked with cars and trucks. A German traffic jam is a peculiar sight: no one honks, no one switches lanes searching for some small, illusory advantage, all trucks remain in the right-hand lane, where they are required to be. The spectacle of sparkling BMWs and Mercedes-

Benzes in the left lane and immaculate trucks in a neat row in the right lane is almost a pleasure to watch. Because everyone in the jam obeys the rules, and believes that everyone else will obey them, too, the cars and trucks move as fast as they can, given the circumstances. But the pretty young German woman behind the wheel of our car doesn't take any pleasure in it. Charlotte huffs and groans at the sight of brake lights stretching into the distance. "It's what I hate more than anything in the world," she says apologetically. "I hate being stuck in traffic."

She pulls from her bag the German translation of Alan Dundes's book. I'd asked her about the title. There is a common German expression, she explains, that translates directly as "lick my ass." To this hearty salutation the common German reply is, "You lick mine first." The German version of Dundes is called *You Lick Mine First.* "Everyone will understand this title," she says. "But this book, I don't know about this."

The last time I'd been in Germany for more than a few days was when I was seventeen years old. I'd traveled across the country with two friends, a bike, and a German phrase book. In my head was a German love song taught to me by an American woman of German descent. So few people spoke English that it was better to assume they did not and deploy whatever German came to hand—which usually meant the love song. And so I assumed on this trip I would need an interpreter. I didn't appreciate how much the Germans had been boning up on their English. The entire population seems to have taken a total-immersion Berlitz course. And on Planet Money, even in Germany, English is the official language. It's the language used for all meetings inside the European Central Bank, for instance, even though the ECB is in Germany, and the only ECB country in which English is even arguably the native tongue is Ireland.

Through a friend of a friend of a friend I'd landed Charlotte, a sweet-natured, keenly intelligent woman in her twenties who was also shockingly steely—how many sweet-natured young women can say "lick my ass" without blushing? She spoke seven languages, including Mandarin and Polish, and was finishing up her master's in Intercultural Misunderstanding, which just has to be Europe's next growth industry. By the time I realized I didn't need her I'd already hired her, and so she had ceased to be my interpreter and become my driver. As my interpreter, she would have been ridiculously overqualified; as my chauffeur she is frankly preposterous. But she'd taken on the job with gusto, going so far as to hunt down an old German translation of Dundes's little book.

And it troubled her. For a start, she refused to believe there was such a thing as a German national character. "No one in my field believes this anymore," she says. "How do you generalize about eighty million people? You can say they are all the same, but why would they be this way? My question about Germans' being anally obsessed is how would this spread? Where would it come from?" Dundes himself actually made a stab at answering the question. He suggested that the unusual swaddling techniques employed by German mothers, which left babies stewing in their own filth for long periods of time, might be responsible for their energetic anality. Charlotte was not buying it. "I've never heard of this," she says.

But just then she spots something and brightens. "Look!" she says. "A German flag." Sure enough, a flag flies over a small house in a distant village. You can spend days in Germany without seeing a flag. Germans aren't allowed to cheer for their team the way other people do. That doesn't mean they don't want to, just that they must disguise what they are doing. "Patriotism," she says, "is still taboo. It's politically incorrect to say, 'I'm proud to be German.'"

The traffic eases, and we're once again flying toward Düsseldorf. The highway looks brand-new, and she guns the rented BMW until the speedometer tops 210 kilometers per hour.

"This is a really good road," I say.

"The Nazis built it," she says. "That's what

people say about Hitler, when they get tired of saying the usual things. Well, at least he built good roads."

BACK IN FEBRUARY 2004 a financial writer in London named Nicholas Dunbar broke the story about some Germans in Düsseldorf, working inside a bank called IKB, who were up to something new. "The name IKB just kept coming up in London with bond salesmen," says Dunbar. "It was like everybody's secret cash cow." Inside the big Wall Street firms there were people whose job it was, when the German customers from Düsseldorf came to London, to get a wad of cash and make sure the Germans got whatever they wanted.

Dunbar's piece appeared in *Risk* magazine and described how this obscure German bank was rapidly turning into Wall Street's biggest customer. IKB had been created back in 1924 to securitize German war reparation payments to the Allies, morphed into a successful lender to midsized German companies, and was now morphing into something else. The bank was partially owned by a German state bank, but was not itself guaranteed by the German government. It was a private German financial enterprise, seemingly on the rise. And it had hired a man named Dirk Röthig, a German with some experience in the United States (he'd worked for

State Street Bank), to do something new and interesting.

With Röthig's help IKB created, in effect, a bank, incorporated in Delaware and listed on the exchange in Dublin, Ireland, called Rhineland Funding. They didn't call it a bank. If they had called it a bank, people might have asked why it was not regulated. They called it a "conduit," a word that had the advantage that no one understood what it meant. Rhineland borrowed money for short periods of time by issuing something called commercial paper. They invested it in longer-term "structured credit," which turned out to be a euphemism for bonds backed by American consumer loans. Many of the same Wall Street investment banks that raised the money for Rhineland (by selling the commercial paper for them) sold Rhineland the bonds backed by the American consumer loans. Rhineland's profits came from the difference between the rate of interest it paid on the money it borrowed and the higher rate of interest it earned on the money it lent through its bond purchases. As IKB guaranteed the entire enterprise, Moody's rating service gave Rhineland its highest rating, enabling Rhineland to borrow money cheaply.

The Germans in Düsseldorf had one critical job: to advise this offshore vehicle they had created about which bonds it should buy. "We are one of the last to get our money out of Rhineland," Röthig told *Risk* magazine, "but we're so confident of our ability to advise it in the right way that we still make a profit." Röthig further explained that IKB had invested in special tools to analyze the complicated bonds, called collateralized debt obligations (CDOs), that Wall Street was now peddling. "I would say it has proven a worthwhile investment because we have not faced a loss so far," he said. In February 2004 all this seemed like a good idea—so good that lots of other German banks copied IKB, and either rented IKB's conduit or set up their own offshore vehicles to buy subprime mortgage bonds. "It sounds like quite a profitable strategy," the man from Moody's who had awarded Rhineland's commercial paper a triple-A rating told *Risk* magazine.

I met Dirk Röthig for lunch at a restaurant in Düsseldorf, on a canal lined with busy shops. From their profitable strategy IKB has announced losses of roughly $15 billion, though their actual losses are probably greater, as German banks are slow to declare anything. Röthig viewed himself, with some justice, more as victim than perpetrator. "I left the bank in December 2005," he says quickly, as he squeezes himself into a small booth. Then he explains.

The idea for the offshore bank had been his. The German management at IKB had taken to it, as he put it, "like a baby takes to candy." He'd created the bank when the market was paying higher returns to bondholders: Rhineland Funding was paid well for the risk it was taking. By the middle of 2005, with the financial markets refusing to see a cloud in the sky, the price of risk had collapsed: the returns on the bonds backed by American consumer loans had collapsed. Röthig says he went to his superiors and argued that, as they were being paid a lot less to take the risk of these bonds, IKB should look elsewhere for profits. "But they had a profit target and they wanted to meet it. To make the same profit with a lower risk spread they simply had to buy more," he says. The management, he adds, did not want to hear his message. "I showed them the market was turning," he says. "I was taking the candy away from the baby, instead of giving it. So I became the enemy." When he left, others left with him, and the investment staff was reduced, but the investment activity boomed. "One-half the number of people with one-third the experience made twice the number of investments," he says. "They were ordered to buy."

He goes on to describe what appeared to be a scrupulous and complicated investment strategy but was actually a mindless, rule-based investment strategy. IKB could "value a CDO down to the last basis point," as one admiring observer told *Risk* magazine in 2004. But in this expertise was a kind of madness. "They would be really anal about, say, which subprime originator went into these CDOs," says Nicholas Dunbar. "They'd say we won't take loans from First Franklin but we will take them from Countrywide. But it didn't matter. They were arguing about bonds that would collapse from one hundred [par] down to two or three [percent of par]. In a sense they were right: they bought the bonds that went to three, rather than to two." As long as the bonds offered up by the Wall Street firms abided by the rules specified by IKB's experts, they got hoovered into the Rhineland Funding portfolio without further inspection. Yet the bonds were becoming radically more risky, because the loans that underpinned them were becoming crazier and crazier. After he left, Röthig explains, IKB had only five investment officers, each in his late twenties, with a couple of years' experience: these were the people on the other end of the bets being handcrafted by Goldman Sachs for its own proprietary trading book, and by other big Wall Street firms for extremely clever hedge funds that wanted to bet against the market for subprime bonds. The IKB portfolio went from $10 billion in 2005 to $20 billion in 2007, Röthig says, "and it would have gotten bigger if they had had more time to buy. They were still buying when the market crashed. They were on their way to thirty billion dollars."

By the middle of 2007 every Wall Street firm, not just Goldman Sachs, realized that the subprime market was collapsing, and tried frantically to get out of their positions. The last buyers *in the entire world,* several people on Wall Street have told me, were these willfully oblivious Germans. That is, the only thing that stopped IKB from losing even more than $15 billion on U.S. subprime loans was that the market ceased to function. Nothing that happened—no fact, no piece of data—was going to alter their approach to investing money.

On the surface the IKB's German bond traders resembled the reckless traders who made similarly stupid bets for Citigroup and Merrill Lynch and Morgan Stanley. Beneath it they were playing an entirely different game. The American bond traders may have sunk their firms by turning a blind eye to the risks in the subprime bond market, but they made a fortune for themselves in the bargain, and have for the most part never been called to account. They were paid to put their firms in jeopardy, and so it is hard to know whether they did it intentionally or not. The German bond traders, on the other hand, had been paid roughly one hundred thousand dollars a year, with, at most, another fifty-thousand-dollar bonus. In general, German bankers were paid peanuts to run the risk that sank their banks, which strongly suggests that they really didn't know what they were doing. But—and here is the strange thing—unlike their American counterparts, they are being treated by the German public as crooks. The former CEO of IKB, Stefan Ortseifen, was given a jail term (since suspended) and has been asked by the bank to return his salary: 805 *thousand* euros.

Dirk Röthig had enjoyed a ringside seat not only to IKB but to the behavior of its imitators, the German state-backed banks, the Landesbanks. And in his view, the border created by modern finance between Anglo-American and German bankers was treacherous. "The intercultural misunderstandings were quite intense," he says, as he tucks into his lobster. "The people in these banks were never spoiled by any Wall Street salesmen. Now there is someone with a platinum American Express credit card who can take them to the Grand Prix in Monaco, takes you to all these places. He has no limit. The Landesbanks were the most boring bankers in Germany so they never got attention like this. And all of a sudden a very smart guy from Merrill Lynch shows up and starts to pay a lot of attention to you. They thought, 'Oh, he just likes me!' " He completes the thought. "The American salespeople are much smarter than the European ones. They play a role much better."

At bottom, he says, the Germans were blind to the possibility that the Americans were playing the game by something other than the official rules. The Germans took the rules at their face value: they looked into the history of triple-A-rated bonds and accepted the official story that triple-A-rated bonds were completely risk-free.

This preternatural love of rules almost for their own sake punctuates German finance as it does German life. As it happens, a story had just broken that a German reinsurance company called Munich Re, back in June 2007, or just before the crash, had sponsored a party for its best producers that offered not just chicken dinners and nearest-to-the-pin golf competitions but a blowout with prostitutes in a public bath. In finance, high or low, this sort of thing is of course not unusual. What was striking was how organized the German event was. The company tied white and yellow and red ribbons to the prostitutes to indicate which ones were available to which men. After each sexual encounter the prostitute received a stamp on her arm to indicate how often she had been used. The Germans didn't just want hookers: they wanted hookers with *rules*.

Perhaps because they were so enamored of the official rules of finance, the Germans proved especially vulnerable to a false idea the rules encouraged: that there is such a thing as a riskless asset. After all, a triple-A rating was supposed to mean "riskless asset." There is no such thing as a riskless asset. The reason an asset pays a return is that it carries risk. But the idea of the riskless asset, which peaked about late 2006, overran the investment world, and the Germans fell for it the hardest. I'd heard about this, too, from people on Wall Street who had dealt with German bond buyers. "You have to go back to the German mentality," one of them had told me. "They say, 'I've ticked all the boxes. There is no risk.' It was form over substance. You work with Germans, and—I can't emphasize this enough—they are not natural risk takers. They are genetically disposed to fucking it up." So long as a bond looked clean on the outside, the Germans allowed it to become as dirty on the inside as Wall Street could make it.

The point Röthig wants to stress to me now is that *it didn't matter* what was on the inside. IKB had to be rescued by a state-owned bank on July 28, 2007. Against capital of roughly $4 billion it had lost more than $15 billion. As it collapsed, the German media wanted to know how many U.S. subprime bonds these German bankers had gobbled up. IKB's CEO, Stefan Ortseifen, said publicly that IKB owned almost no subprime bonds at all—which is why he's now charged with misleading investors. "He was telling the truth," says Röthig. "He didn't think he owned any subprime. They weren't able to give any correct numbers of the amount of subprime they had, because they didn't know. The IKB monitoring systems did not make a distinction between subprime and prime mortgages. And that's why it happened." Back in 2005, Röthig says, he proposed to build a system to track more precisely what loans were behind the complex bonds they were buying from Wall Street firms, but IKB's management didn't want to spend the money. "I told them you have a portfolio of twenty billion dollars, you are making two hundred million dollars a year and you are denying me six point five million. But they didn't want to do it."

FOR THE THIRD time in as many days we cross the border without being able to see it, and spend twenty minutes trying to work out if we are in East or West Germany. Charlotte was born and raised in the East German city of Leipzig, but she is no less uncertain than I am about which former country we are in. "You just would not know anymore unless you are told," she says. "They have to put up a sign to mark it." A landscape once scarred by trenches and barbed wire and minefields exhibits not so much as a ripple. On the outside, at least, it's perfectly clean. Somewhere near this former border we pull off the road into a gas station. It has three pumps in a narrow channel without space to maneuver or to pass. The three drivers filling their gas tanks need to do it together, and move along together, for if any one driver dawdles, everyone else must wait. No driver dawdles. The German drivers service their cars with the efficiency of a pit crew. Precisely because the arrangement is so archaic, Charlotte guesses we must still be in West Germany. "You would never find this kind of gas station in East Germany," she says. "Everything in East Germany is new." She also claims she can guess at sight whether a person, and especially a man, is from the east or the west. "West Germans are *much* prouder. They stand straight. East Germans are more likely to slouch. West Germans think East Germans are lazy."

"East Germans are the Greeks of Germany," I say.

"Be careful," she says.

From Düsseldorf we drive to Leipzig, and from Leipzig we hop a train to Hamburg to find the mud wrestling. Along the way she humors me by parsing her native tongue for signs of anality. "*Kackwurst* is the term for feces," she says grudgingly. "It literally means shit sausage. And it's horrible. When I see sausages I can't think of anything else." She thinks a moment. "*Bescheissen*: someone shit on you. *Klugscheisser*: an intelligence shitter.

"If you have a lot of money," she continues, "you are said to shit money: *Geldscheisser*." She rips a handful of other examples off the top of her head, a little shocked by how fertile is this line of thinking, before she says, "And if you find yourself in a bad situation, you say, '*Die Kacke ist am dampfen*: the shit is steaming.'" She stops and appears to realize she is encouraging a theory of German national character.

"It's just in the words," she says.

"Sure it is."

"It doesn't mean it applies."

Outside of Hamburg we stopped for lunch at a farm owned by a man named Wilhelm Nölling, a German economist now in his seventies but with the kick and bite of a much younger man. He has the chiseled features and silver hair of a patrician but the vocal cords of a bleacher bum. "The Greeks want us to pay their lunch!" he bellows, as he gives me a tour of his private goat pen. "That is why they are rioting in the streets! Baaa!" Back when the idea of the euro was being bandied about, Nölling had been a governor of the Bundesbank. From the moment the discussion turned serious he has railed against the euro. He'd written one mournful pamphlet called "Good-bye to the Deutsche Mark?" and another, more declarative pamphlet called "The Euro: A Journey to Hell." Together with three other prominent German economists and financial leaders he'd filed a lawsuit, still wending its way through the German courts, challenging the euro on constitutional grounds. Just before the deutsche mark got scrapped, Nölling had argued to the Bundesbank that they should just keep all the notes. "I said, 'Don't shred it!' " he now says with great gusto, leaping out of an armchair in the living room of his farmhouse. "I said, 'Pile it all up, put it in a room, in case we need it later!' "

He finds himself stuck: he knows that he is engaged in an exercise futile and pointless. "Can you turn this back?" he says. "We know we can't turn this back. If they say, 'Okay, we were wrong, you were right,' what do you do? That is the hundred-thousand-million-dollar question." He thinks he knows what should be done but doesn't think Germans are capable of doing it. The idea he and his fellow dissident German economists have cooked up is to split the European Union in two for financial purposes. One euro, a kind of second-string currency, would be issued for, and used by, the deadbeat countries—Greece, Portugal, Spain, Italy, and so on. The first-string euro would be used by "the homogenous countries, the ones you can rely on." He lists these reliable countries: Germany, Austria, Belgium, the Netherlands, Finland, and (he hesitates for a second over this) France.

"Are you sure the French belong?"

"We discussed this," he says seriously. They decided that for social reasons you couldn't really exclude the French. It was just too awkward.

As he presided over the Maastricht treaty,

which created the euro, the French prime minister François Mitterrand is rumored to have said privately that yoking Germany to the rest of Europe in this way was sure to lead to imbalances, and the imbalances were certain to lead to some crisis, but by the time the crisis struck he'd be dead and gone—and others would sort it out. Even if Mitterrand didn't say exactly that, it's the sort of thing he should have said, as he surely thought it. At the time it was obvious to a lot of people, and not only Bundesbank governors, that these countries did not belong together.

But then how did people who seem as intelligent and successful and honest and well organized as the Germans allow themselves to be drawn into such a mess? In their financial affairs they'd ticked all the little boxes to ensure that the contents of the bigger box were not rotten, and yet ignored the overpowering stench wafting from the big box. Nölling felt the problem had its roots in German national character. "We entered Maastricht because they had these *rules,*" he says, as we move off to his kitchen and plates heaped with the white asparagus Germans take such pride in growing. "We were talked into this under false pretenses. Germans are, by and large, gullible people. They trust and believe. They *like* to trust. They *like* to believe."

If the deputy finance minister has a sign on his

wall reminding him to see the point of view of others, here is perhaps why. Others do not behave as Germans do: others *lie*. In this financial world of deceit Germans are natives on a protected island who have not been inoculated against the virus carried by visitors. The same instincts that allowed them to trust Wall Street bond salesmen also allowed them to trust the French, when they promised there would be no bailouts, and the Greeks, when they swore that their budget was balanced. That is one theory. Another is that they trusted so easily because they didn't care enough about the cost of being wrong, as it came with certain benefits. For the Germans the euro isn't just a currency. It's a device for flushing away the past. It's another Holocaust Memorial. The Greeks may have German public opinion polls running against them, but deeper forces run in their favor.

In any case, if you are obsessed with cleanliness and order yet harbor a secret fascination with filth and chaos, you are bound to get into some kind of trouble. There is no such thing as clean without dirt. There is no such thing as purity without impurity. The interest in one implies an interest in the other. The young German woman who had driven me back and forth across Germany exhibits interest in neither, and it's hard to say whether she is an exception or a new rule. Still, she marches dutifully into the world's largest red-light district, seeking out a lot of seedy-looking German men to ask them where she might find a female mud wrestling show. Even now she continues to find new and surprising ways in which Germans find meaning in filth. "*Scheisse glänzt nicht, wenn man sie poliert*: Shit won't shine, even if you polish it," she says, as we pass the Funky Pussy Club. "*Scheissegal*: it just means 'I don't give a shit.' " She laughs. "That's an oxymoron in Germany, right?"

The night is young and the Reeperbahn is hopping: it's the closest thing I've seen in Germany to a mob scene. Hawkers lean against sex clubs and sift likely customers from the passing crowds. Women who are almost pretty beckon men who are clearly tempted. We pass several times the same corporate logo, of a pair of stick figures engaged in anal sex. Charlotte spots it and remembers that a German band, Rammstein, was arrested in the United States for simulating anal sex on stage while performing a song called "Bück Dich" (Bend Over). But on she charges, asking old German men where to find the dirt. At length she finds a definitive answer, from a German who has worked here for decades. "The last one shut down years ago," he says. "It was too expensive."

# V

## TOO FAT TO FLY

On August 5, 2011, moments after the U.S. government watched a rating agency lower its credit rating for the first time in American history, the market for U.S. Treasury bonds soared. Four days later, the interest rates paid by the U.S. government on its new ten-year bonds had fallen to the lowest level on record, 2.04 percent. The price of gold rose right alongside the price of U.S. Treasury bonds, but the prices of virtually all other stocks and bonds in rich Western countries went into a free fall. The net effect of a major U.S. rating agency's saying that the U.S. government was less likely than before to repay its debts was to lower the cost of borrowing for the U.S. government and to raise it for everyone else. This told you a lot of what you needed to know about the ability of the U.S. government to live beyond its means: it had, for the moment, a blank check. The shakier the United States government appeared, up to some faraway point, the more cheaply it would be able to borrow. It wasn't exposed yet to the same vicious cycle that threatened the financial life of European countries: a moment of doubt leads to higher borrowing costs, which leads to greater doubt, and even higher borrowing costs, and so on until you become Greece. The fear that the United States might actually not pay back the money it had borrowed was still unreal.

On December 19, 2010, the television news program *60 Minutes* aired a thirteen-minute piece about U.S. state and local finances. The correspondent Steve Kroft interviewed a private Wall Street analyst named Meredith Whitney, who, back in 2007, had gone from being obscure to famous when she correctly suggested that Citigroup's losses in U.S. subprime bonds were far bigger than anyone imagined, and predicted the bank would be forced to cut its dividend. The *60 Minutes* segment noted that U.S. state and local governments faced a collective annual deficit of roughly half a trillion dollars, and noted another trillion-and-a-half-dollar gap between what the governments owed retired workers and the money they had on hand to pay them. Whitney pointed out that even these numbers were unreliable, and probably optimistic, as the states did a poor job of providing information about their finances to the public. New Jersey governor Chris Christie concurred with her and added, "At this point, if it's worse, what's the difference?" The bill owed by American states to retired American workers was so large that it couldn't be paid, whatever the amount. At the end of the piece Kroft asked Whitney what she thought about the ability and willingness of the American states to repay their debts. She didn't see a real risk that the states would default, because the states had the ability to push their problems down to counties and cities. But at these lower levels of government, where American life was lived, she thought there would be serious problems. "You could see fifty to a hundred sizable defaults, maybe more," she said. A minute later Kroft returned to her to ask her when people should start worrying about a crisis in local finances. "It'll be something to worry about within the next twelve months," she said.

That prophecy turned out to be self-fulfilling: people started worrying about U.S. municipal finance the minute the words were out of her mouth. The next day the municipal bond market tanked. It kept falling right through the next month. It fell so far, and her prediction received so much attention, that money managers who had put clients into municipal bonds felt compelled to hire more people to analyze states and cities, to prove her wrong. (One of them called it "The Meredith Whitney Municipal Bond Analyst Full Employment Act.") Inside the financial world a new literature was born, devoted to persuading readers that Meredith Whitney didn't know what she was talking about. She was vulnerable to the charge: up until the moment she appeared on *60 Minutes* she had, so far as anyone knew, no experience at all of U.S. municipal finance. Many of the articles attacking her accused her of making a very specific forecast—as many as a hundred defaults within a year!—that had failed to materialize. (Sample Bloomberg News headline: MEREDITH WHITNEY LOSES CREDIBILITY AS MUNI DEFAULTS FALL 60%.) The whirlwind thrown up by the brief market panic sucked in everyone who was anywhere near municipal finance. The nonpartisan, dispassionate, sober-minded Center on Budget and Policy Priorities, in Washington, D.C., even released a statement saying that there was a "mistaken impression that drastic and immediate measures are needed to avoid an imminent fiscal meltdown." This was treated in news accounts as a response to Meredith Whitney, as she was the only one in sight who could be accused of having made such a prediction.

But that's not at all what she had said: her words were being misrepresented so that her message might be more easily attacked. "She was referring to the complacency of the ratings agencies and investment advisers who say there is nothing to worry about," said a person at *60 Minutes* who reviewed the transcripts of the interview for me, to make sure I had heard what I thought I had heard. "She says there is something to worry about, and it will be apparent to everyone in the next twelve months."

Whatever else she had done, Meredith Whitney had found the pressure point in American finance: the fear that American cities would not pay back the money they had borrowed. The market for municipal bonds, unlike the market for U.S. government bonds, spooked easily. American cities and states were susceptible to the same cycle of doom that had forced Greece to seek help from the International Monetary Fund. All it took to create doubt, and raise borrowing costs for states and cities, was for a woman with no standing in the municipal bond market to utter a few sentences on television. That was the amazing thing: she had offered nothing to back up her statement. She'd written a massive, detailed report on state and local finances, but no one except a handful of her clients had any idea what was in it. "If I was a real nasty hedge fund guy," one hedge fund manager put it to me, "I'd sit back and say, 'This is a herd of cattle that can be stampeded.'"

What Meredith Whitney was trying to say was more interesting than what she was accused of saying. She didn't actually care all that much about the municipal bond market, or how many cities were likely to go bankrupt. The municipal bond market was a dreary backwater. As she put it, "Who cares about the stinking muni bond market?" The only reason she had stumbled into that market was that she had come to view the U.S. national economy as a collection of regional economies. To understand the regional economies, she had to understand how state and local governments were likely to behave; and to understand this she needed to understand their finances. Thus she had spent two unlikely years researching state and local finance. "I didn't have a plan to do this," she said. "Not one of my clients asked for it. I only looked at this because I needed to understand it myself. How it started was with a question: how can GDP [gross domestic product] estimates be so high when the states that outperformed the U.S. economy during the boom were now underperforming the U.S. economy—and they were twenty-two percent of that economy?" It was a good question.

From 2002 to 2008, the states had piled up debts right alongside their citizens': their level of indebtedness, as a group, had almost doubled, and state spending had grown by two-thirds. In that time they had also systematically underfunded their pension plans and other future liabilities by a total of nearly $1.5 trillion. In response, perhaps, the pension money that they had set aside was invested in ever-riskier assets. In 1980 only 23 percent of state pension money had been invested in the stock market; by 2008 the number had risen to 60 percent. To top it all off, these pension funds were pretty much all assuming they could earn 8 percent on the money they had to invest, at a time when the Federal Reserve was promising to keep interest rates at zero. Toss in underfunded health care plans, a reduction in federal dollars available to the states, and the depression in tax revenues caused by a soft economy, and you were looking at multi-trillion-dollar holes that could only be dealt with in one of two ways—massive cutbacks on public services or a default—or both. She thought default unlikely, at least at the state level, because the state could bleed the cities of money to pay off its bonds. The cities were where the pain would be felt most intensely. "The scary thing about state treasurers," she said "is that they don't know the financial situation in their own municipalities."

"How do you know that?"

"Because I asked them!"

All states may have been created equal, but they were equal no longer. The states that had enjoyed the biggest boom were now facing the biggest busts. "How does the United States emerge from the credit crisis?" Whitney asked herself. "I was convinced—because the credit crisis had been so different from region to region—that it would emerge with new regional strengths and weaknesses. Companies are more likely to flourish in the stronger states; the individuals will go to where the jobs are. Ultimately, the people will follow the companies." The country, she thought, might organize itself increasingly into zones of financial security and zones of financial crisis. And the more clearly people understood which zones were which, the more friction there would be between the two. ("Indiana is going to be like, 'NFW I'm bailing out New Jersey.'") As more and more people grasped which places had serious financial problems and which did not, the problems would only increase. "Those who have money and can move do so," Whitney wrote in her report to her Wall Street clients, "those without money and who cannot move do not, and ultimately rely more on state and local assistance. It becomes effectively a 'tragedy of the commons.'"

The point of Meredith Whitney's investigation, in her mind, was not to predict defaults in the municipal bond market. It was to compare the states to each other so that they might be ranked. She wanted to get a sense of who in America was likely to play the role of the Greeks, and who the Germans. Of who was strong, and who weak. In the process she had, in effect, unearthed America's scariest financial places.

"So what's the scariest state?" I asked her.

She only had to think for about two seconds.

"California."

AT SEVEN O'CLOCK one summer morning I pedaled a five-thousand-dollar titanium-frame mountain bike rented in anxiety the previous evening down the Santa Monica beach road to the corner where Arnold Schwarzenegger had asked me to meet him. He turned up right on time, driving a black Cadillac SUV with a handful of crappy old jalopy bikes racked to the back. I wore the closest I could find to actual bicycle gear; he wore a green fleece, shorts, and soft beige slipperlike shoes that suggested both a surprising indifference to his own appearance and a security in his own manhood. His hair was still vaguely in a shape left by a pillow, and his eyelids drooped, though he swore he'd been up for an hour and a half reading newspapers. After reading the newspapers, this is what the former governor of California often does: ride his bike for cardio, then hit the weight room.

He hauls a bike off the back of the car, hops on, and takes off down an already busy Ocean Avenue. He wears no bike helmet, runs red lights, and rips past DO NOT ENTER signs without seeming to notice them, and up one-way streets. When he wants to cross three lanes of fast traffic he doesn't so much as glance over his shoulder but just sticks out his hand and follows it, assuming that whatever is behind him will stop. His bike has at least ten speeds but he has just two: zero, and pedaling as fast as he can. Inside half a mile he's moving fast enough that wind-induced tears course down his cheeks.

He's got to be one of the world's most recognizable people, but he doesn't appear to worry that anyone will recognize him, and no one does. It may be that people who get out of bed at dawn to jog and Rollerblade and race-walk are too interested in what they are doing to break their trance. Or it may be that he's taking them by surprise. He has no entourage, not even a bodyguard. His economic adviser, David Crane, and his media adviser, Adam Mendelsohn, who came along for the ride just because it sounded fun, are now somewhere far behind him. Anyone paying attention would think, That guy might look like Arnold but it can't possibly be Arnold because Arnold would never be out alone on a bike at seven in the morning, trying to commit suicide. It isn't until he is forced to stop at a red light that he makes meaningful contact with the public. A woman pushing a baby stroller and talking on a cell phone crosses the street right in front of him, and does a double take. "Oh . . . my . . . God," she gasps into her phone. "It's Bill Clinton!" She's not ten feet away but she keeps talking to the phone, as if the man is unreal. "I'm here with Bill Clinton."

"It's one of those guys who has had a sex scandal," says Arnold, smiling.

"Wait . . . wait," says the woman to her phone. "Maybe it's not Bill Clinton."

Before she can make a positive identification the light is green, and we're off.

His life has been a series of carefully staged experiences. He himself has no staged presentation of it, however. He is fresh, alive, and improvisational: I'm not sure even he knows what he will do next. He's not exactly humble, but then if I had lived the life he's lived I'm not sure I would be, either, though I might try to fake humility more often than he does, which is roughly never. What saves him from self-absorption, aside from a natural curiosity, is a genuine lack of interest in personal reflection. He lives the same way he rides his bike, paying far more attention to what's ahead than what's behind. In office, he kept no journal of any sort. I find it amazing, but he now says he didn't so much as scribble little notes that might later be used to reconstruct his experience and his feelings about it. "Why would I do that?" he says. "It's kind of like you come home and your wife asks you about your day. I've done it once and I don't want to do it again." What he wanted to do after a long day of being governor, more or less, was to lift weights.

We're just a couple of miles in when he zips around a corner and into a narrow alleyway just off Venice Beach. He's humoring me; I've been pestering him about what it was like for him when he first arrived in America, back in 1968, with little money, less English, really nothing but his lats, pecs, traps, and abs, for which there was no obvious market. He stops beside a tall brick wall. It surrounds what might once have been an impressive stone house that now just looks old and bleak and empty. The wall is what interests him, because he built it, forty-three years ago, right after he had arrived and started to train on Muscle Beach. "Franco [Columbu, like Schwarzenegger a former Mr. Olympia] and I made money this way. In bodybuilding there was no money. Here we were world champions of this little subculture, and we did this to eat. Franco ran the business. I mixed the cement and knocked things down with the sledgehammer."

Before he stumbled while running downhill with a refrigerator strapped to his back, Columbu was the front-runner in the 1977 contest for the title of the World's Strongest Man; so there was some distinction in being hired by his operation, as Schwarzenegger was, to be the muscle. They had a routine. Franco would play the unreliable Italian, Arnold the sober German. Before they cut any deal they'd scream at each other in German in front of the customer until the customer would finally ask what was going on. Arnold would turn to the customer and explain, *Oh, he's Italian, and you know how they are. He wants to charge you*

*more, but I think we can do it cheaply.*
Schwarzenegger would then name a not-so-cheap price. "And the customer," he says now, laughing, "he would always say, 'Arnold, you're such a nice guy! So honest!' It was selling, you know."

He surveys his handiwork. "It'll be here for a thousand years," he says, then points out some erosion on the top. "I said to Franco we ought to come back and fix the top. You know, to show it was guaranteed for life."

A poor kid from a small village in Austria, the son of a former Nazi, hops on a plane to America, starts out laying bricks, and winds up running the state and becoming one of America's most prominent political leaders. From post to wire the race takes less than thirty-five years. I couldn't help but ask the obvious question.

"If someone had told you when you were building this wall that you would wind up governor of California, what would you have said?"

"That would be all right," he said, not exactly catching my drift.

"As a boy," I said, taking another tack, "did you believe you'd lead something other than an ordinary life?"

"Yes." He didn't miss a beat.

"Why?"

"I don't know.

"*No one* has had this kind of crazy, wild ride,"

he says, as we speed away from the brick wall, but in a tone that suggests the ride was an accident. "I was influenced a lot by America," he said. "The giant six-lane highways, the Empire State Building, the risk taking." He still remembers vividly the America he heard and read about as a boy in Austria: everything about it was *big*. The only reason he set out to grow himself some big muscles was that he thought it might be a ticket to America.

If there had not been a popular movement to remove a sitting governor, and the chance to run for governor without having to endure a party primary, he never would have bothered. "The recall happens and people are asking me: what are you going to do?" he says, dodging vagrants and joggers along the beach bike path. "I thought about it but decided I wasn't going to do it. I told Maria I wasn't running. I told everyone I wasn't running. I *wasn't* running." Then, in the middle of the recall madness, *Terminator 3: Rise of the Machines* opened. As the movie's leading machine he was expected to appear on *The Tonight Show* to promote it. En route he experienced a familiar impulse—the impulse to do something out of the ordinary. "I just thought, This will freak everyone out," he says. "It'll be so funny. I'll announce that I am running. I told Leno I was running. And two months later I was governor." He looks over at me, pedaling as fast as I can to keep up with him, and laughs. "What the fuck is *that?*"

We're now off the beach and on the surface roads, and the traffic is already heavy. He veers left, across four lanes of traffic, arrives on the other side, and says, "All these people are asking me, 'What's your plan? Who's on your staff?' I didn't have a plan. I didn't have a staff. I wasn't running until I went on Jay Leno."

His view of his seven years trying to run the state of California, like the views of his closest associates, can be summarized as follows. He came to power accidentally, but not without ideas about what he wanted to do. At his core he thought government had become more problem than solution: an institution run less for the benefit of the people than for the benefit of politicians and other public employees. He behaved pretty much as Americans seem to imagine the ideal politician should behave: he made bold decisions without looking at polls; he didn't sell favors; he treated his opponents fairly; he was quick to acknowledge his mistakes and to learn from them, and so on. He was the rare elected official who believed, with some reason, that he had nothing to lose, and behaved accordingly. When presented with the chance to pursue an agenda that violated his own narrow political self-interest for the sake of the public interest, he tended to leap at it. "There were a lot

of times when we said, 'You just can't do that,'"
says his former chief of staff, Susan Kennedy, a
lifelong Democrat, whose hiring was one of those
things a Republican governor was not supposed
to do. "He was always like, 'I don't care.' Ninety
percent of the time it was a good thing."

Two years into his tenure, in mid-2005, he'd
tried everything he could think of to persuade
individual California state legislators to vote
against the short-term desires of their constituents
for the greater long-term good of all. "To me
there were shocking moments," he says. Having
sped past a DO NOT ENTER sign, we are now
flying through intersections without pausing. I
can't help but notice that, if we weren't breaking
the law by going the wrong way down a one-way
street, we'd be breaking the law by running stop
signs. "When you want to do pension reform for
the prison guards," he says, "and all of a sudden
*the Republicans* are all lined up against you. It
was really incredible and it happened over and
over: people would say to me, 'Yes, this is the
best idea! I would love to vote for it! But if I vote
for it some interest group is going to be angry
with me, so I won't do it.' I couldn't believe
people could actually say that. You have soldiers
dying in Iraq and Afghanistan, and they didn't
want to risk their political lives by doing the right
thing."

He came into office with boundless faith in the

American people—after all, they had elected him—and figured he could always appeal directly to them. That was his trump card, and he played it. In November 2005 he called a special election that sought votes on four reforms: limiting state spending, putting an end to the gerrymandering of legislative districts, limiting public employee union spending on elections, and lengthening the time it took for public school teachers to get tenure. All four propositions addressed, directly or indirectly, the state's large and growing financial mess. All four were defeated; the votes weren't even close. From then until the end of his time in office he was effectively gelded: the legislators now knew that the people who had elected them to behave exactly the way they were already behaving were not going to undermine them when appealed to directly. The people of California might be irresponsible, but at least they were consistent.

A compelling book called *California Crackup* describes this problem more generally. It's written by a pair of journalists and nonpartisan think tank scholars, Joe Mathews and Mark Paul, and they explain, among other things, why Arnold Schwarzenegger's experience as governor was going to be unlike any other experience in his career: he was never going to win. California had organized itself, not accidentally, into highly partisan legislative districts. It elected highly partisan people to office and then required these people to reach a two-thirds majority to enact any new tax or meddle with big spending decisions. On the off chance that they found some common ground, it could be pulled out from under them by voters through the initiative process. Throw in term limits—no elected official now serves in California government long enough to fully understand it—and you have a recipe for generating maximum contempt for elected officials. Politicians are elected to get things done and are prevented by the system from doing it, leading the people to grow even more disgusted with them. "The vicious cycle of contempt," as Mark Paul calls it. California state government was designed mainly to maximize the likelihood that voters will continue to despise the people they elect.

But when you look below the surface, he adds, the system is actually very good at giving Californians what they want. "What all the polls show," says Paul, "is that people want services and not to pay for them. And that's exactly what they have now got." As much as they claimed to despise their government, the citizens of California shared its defining trait: a need for debt. The average Californian, in 2011, had debts of $78,000 against an income of $43,000. The behavior was unsustainable, but, in its way, for the people, it works brilliantly. For their leaders, even in the short term, it works less well. They ride into office on great false hopes and quickly discover they can do nothing to justify those hopes.

In Paul's view, Arnold Schwarzenegger had been the best test to date of the notion that the problem with California politics was personal; that all the system needed to fix itself was an independent-minded leader willing to rise above petty politics and exert the will of the people. "The recall was, in and of itself, an effort by the people to say that a new governor—a different person—could solve the problem," says Paul. "He tried every different way of dealing with the crisis in services. He tried to act like a Republican. He tried to act like a Democrat. He tried making nice with the legislature. When that didn't work he called them girlie men. When that didn't work he went directly to the people. And the people voted against his proposals."

The experiment hadn't been a complete failure. As governor, Schwarzenegger was able to accomplish a few important things—reforming worker compensation, enabling open primaries, and, at the very end, ensuring that legislative districts would be drawn by an impartial committee rather than by the legislature. But on most issues, and on virtually everything having to do with how the state raised and spent money, he lost. In his first term Schwarzenegger had set out to cut spending and found he could cut only the things that the state actually needed. Near the end of his second term, he managed to pass a slight tax increase, after he talked four Republicans into creating the supermajority necessary for doing so. Every one of them lost his seat in the next election. He'd taken office in 2003 with approval ratings pushing 70 percent and what appeared to be a mandate to fix California's money problems; he'd left in 2011 with approval ratings below 25 percent, having fixed very little. "I was operating under the common sense kind of thing," he says now. "It was the voters who recalled Gray Davis. It was the voters who elected me. So it will be the voters who hand me the tools to do the job. But the other side was successful enough for the voters to take the tools away."

David Crane, his economic adviser—at that moment, rapidly receding into the distance—could itemize the result: a long list of depressing government financial statistics. The pensions of state employees ate up twice as much of the budget when Schwarzenegger left office as they did when he arrived, for instance. The officially recognized gap between what the state would owe its workers and what it had on hand to pay them was roughly $105 billion, but that, thanks to accounting gimmicks, was probably only about half the real number. "This year the state will directly spend thirty-two billion dollars on employee pay and benefits, up sixty-five percent over the past ten years," says Crane later. "Compare that to state spending on higher education [down 5 percent], health and human services [up just 5 percent], and parks and recreation [flat], all crowded out in large part by fast-rising employment costs." Crane was a lifelong Democrat with no particular hostility to government. But the more he'd looked into the details, the more shocking he found them to be. In 2010, for instance, the state spent $6 billion on fewer than 30,000 guards and other prison system employees. A prison guard who started his career at the age of forty-five could retire after five years with a pension that very nearly equaled his former salary. The head parole psychiatrist for the California prison system was California's highest-paid public employee; in 2010 he'd made $838,706. The same fiscal year that the state spent $6 billion on prisons, it had invested just $4.7 billion in its higher education—that is, 33 campuses with 670,000 students. Over the past thirty years the state's share of the budget for the University of California had fallen from 30 percent to 11 percent, and it was about to fall a lot more. In 1980 a Cal student paid $776 a year in tuition; in 2011 he would pay $13,218. Everywhere you turned, the long-term future of the state was being sacrificed.

This same set of facts, and the narrative it

suggested, would throw an ordinary man into depression. He might conclude that he lived in a society that was ungovernable. After seven years of trying and mostly failing to run California, Schwarzenegger is persuasively not depressed. "You have to realize the thing was so much fun!" he says. "We had a great time! There were times of frustration. There were times of disappointment. But if you want to live rather than just exist, you want the drama." As we roll to a stop very near the place on the beach where he began his American bodybuilding career, he says, "You have to step back and say, 'I was elected under odd circumstances. And I'm going out in odd circumstances.' You can't have it both ways. You can't be a spoiled brat."

The odd circumstances were the never-ending financial crises. He'd come to power in the bust after the Internet bubble; he'd left in the bust after the housing bubble. Before and after our bike ride, I had sat down with him to get his view of this second event. It was in the middle of 2007, he said, when he first noticed something was not quite right in the California economy. He'd been finishing up budget negotiations and arrived at a number, however phony, where the budget could be declared balanced. An aide walked into his office to give him a heads-up: the tax receipts for that month were less than expected. "We were all of a sudden short three hundred million dollars in revenue for the month," says Schwarzenegger. "I somehow felt, Uh-oh. Because there was something in the air." Soon after that he visited the George W. Bush White House, where he gave a talk that was, as ever, upbeat. "At the end of it this guy—he was the guy who was in charge of housing, I forgot the name. Great guy. For some reason or other he was very honest with me. I don't know why. He probably didn't think I'd go out and blab, which I didn't. He says, 'That was a great speech you gave, but we're heading to a major problem.' I said, 'What do you mean?' He said, 'I looked at some of the numbers, and it's going to be ugly.' That's all he said. He wouldn't elaborate." A housing price decline in the United States meant a housing price collapse in California; and a housing price collapse in California meant an economic collapse, and a decline in tax revenues. "The next month our revenues came in short six hundred million dollars. By December we were short a billion."

The hope that California would generate the tax revenues needed to pay for even newly reduced services vanished. "This crisis consumed the last three years," says Schwarzenegger. "All of a sudden you are pissing off everyone. The parks don't get money and all of a sudden everyone is in love with parks. People pay attention so much to how does it affect them immediately: that's just the way the human mind works."

How the further degradation of public services affected people immediately would not have been immediately obvious to a governor sitting in Sacramento. As Meredith Whitney had pointed out, the state has great ability to paper over its financial problems by pushing them down to cities. In May 2011, to take just the most cinematic of countless examples, the U.S. Supreme Court upheld a ruling that California's prison conditions constituted cruel and unusual punishment and violated the Eighth Amendment. The ruling ordered the state either to build more prisons or to release thirty thousand inmates. The state—still overpaying its prison guards—has chosen to release the prisoners and, with them, their social cost. There will probably be more crime, and heavier dependency on local public services, but it must be paid for by local communities. At some point in our talks I had asked Schwarzenegger how much time he had spent, as governor, grappling with the on-the-ground local implications of the big state crisis. The question pretty clearly bored him. "I'm not into the local stuff," he'd said. "I was born for the world."

ABOUT AN HOUR into the weekly meeting of the San Jose City Council I find myself wishing that I, too, was born for the world. A hundred citizens yawn and text as the council honors National

Farmer's Market Week; the few people who seemed to be paying attention get up and leave after the honor is bestowed. The council commemorates August 7 as Assyrian Martyrs Day, "honoring the massacre of three thousand people in August 1933, and recognizing 2,000 years of persecution of Assyrian Christians." Maybe thirty people turn their attention from their cell phones to the ceremony but then they, too, rise and exit the chamber. A mere handful of people are left to hear the San Jose city manager offer the latest bleak financial news: the state of California was clawing back tens of millions of dollars more, and "one hundred and forty employees have been separated from the city." (New times call for new euphemisms.) A pollster presents his finding that, no matter how the question is phrased, the citizens of San Jose are unlikely to approve any ballot measure that raises taxes. A numbers guy gets to his feet and explains that the investment returns in the city's pension plan are not likely to be anything like as high as was assumed. In addition to there not being enough money in this particular pot to begin with, the pot is failing to expand as fast as everyone had hoped, and so the gap between what the city's employees are entitled to and what will exist is even greater than previously imagined. The council then votes to postpone, for six weeks, a vote on whether to declare the city's budget a "public emergency," and thus to give to the mayor, Chuck Reed, new powers.

In between each motion an obese man not so much dressed as enshrouded in blue jean overalls maximizes his right to be heard for five minutes on every subject: over and again he rises from the front row of the audience, waddles to the podium, and delivers sophisticated-sounding but incomprehensible critiques of everything. *"The absolute reduction in competence of government is predicated on what happened today . . ."*

The relationship between the people and their money in California is such that you can pluck almost any city at random and enter a crisis. San Jose has the highest per capita income of any city in the United States, after New York. It has the highest credit rating of any city in California with a population over 250,000. It is one of the few cities in America with a triple-A rating from Moody's and Standard & Poor's, but only because its bondholders have the power to compel the city to levy a tax on property owners to pay off the bonds. The city itself is not all that far from being bankrupt.

It's late afternoon when I meet Mayor Chuck Reed, in his office at the top of city hall tower. The crowd below has just begun to chant. The public employees, as usual, are protesting him. Reed is so used to it that he hardly notices. He's a former air force fighter pilot and Vietnam veteran with an intellectual bent and the clipped manner of a midwestern farmer. He has a master's degree from Princeton, a law degree from Stanford, and a lifelong interest in public policy. Still, he presents less as the mayor of a big city in California than as a hard-bitten, upstanding sheriff of a small town who doesn't want any trouble. Elected to the city council in 2000, he became mayor six years later; in 2010, he was reelected with 77 percent of the vote. He's a Democrat, but at this point it doesn't much matter which party he belongs to, or what his ideological leanings are, or for that matter how popular he is with the people of San Jose. He's got a problem so big that it overwhelms ordinary politics: the city owes so much more money than it can afford to pay to its employees that it could cut its debts in half and still wind up broke. "I did a calculation of cost per public employee," he says, as we settle in. "We're not as bad as Greece, I don't think."

The problem, he explains, predates the most recent financial crisis. "Hell, I was here. I know how it started. It started in the 1990s with the Internet boom. We live near rich people, so we thought we were rich." San Jose's budget, like the budget of any city, turns on the pay of public safety workers: the police and firefighters now eat 75 percent of all discretionary spending. The Internet boom created both great expectations for public employees and tax revenues to meet them. In its negotiations with unions the city was required to submit to binding arbitration, which works for police officers and firefighters just as it does for Major League Baseball players. Each side of any pay dispute makes its best offer, and a putatively neutral judge picks one of them. There is no meeting in the middle: the judge simply rules for one side or the other. Each side thus has an incentive to be reasonable, for the less reasonable they are, the less likely it is that the judge will favor their proposal. The problem with binding arbitration for police officers and firefighters, says Reed, is that the judges are not neutral. "They tend to be labor lawyers who favor the unions," he says, "and so the city does anything it can to avoid the process." And what politician wants to spat publicly with police officers and firefighters?

Over the past decade the city of San Jose had repeatedly caved to the demands of its public safety unions. In practice this meant that when the police or fire department of any neighboring city struck a better deal for itself, it became a fresh argument for improving the pay of San Jose police and fire. The effect was to make the sweetest deal cut by public safety workers with any city in northern California the starting point for the next round of negotiations for every other city. The departments also used each other to score debating points. For instance, back in 2002, the San Jose police union cut a three-year deal that raised police officers' pay by 10 percent over the contract. Soon afterward, the San Jose firefighters cut a better deal for themselves, including a pay raise of 23 percent. The police felt robbed and complained mightily until the city council crafted a deal that handed them 5 percent more pay in exchange for training to fight terrorists. "We got famous for our antiterrorist training pay," explains one city official. Eventually the antiterrorist training stopped; the police just kept the extra pay, with benefits. "Our police and firefighters will earn more in retirement than they did when they were working," says Reed. "There used to be an argument that you have to give us money or we can't afford to live in the city. Now the more you pay them the less likely they are to live in the city, because they can afford to leave. It's staggering. When did we go from giving people sick leave to letting them accumulate it and cash it in for hundreds of thousands of dollars when they are done working? There's a corruption here. It's not just a financial corruption. It's a corruption of the attitude of public service."

When he was elected to the city council in 2000, Reed says, "I hadn't even thought about pensions. I can't say I said, 'Here is my plan.' I never thought about this stuff. It never came up."

It wasn't until San Diego flirted with bankruptcy, in 2002, that he wondered about San Jose's finances. He began to investigate the matter. "That's when I realized there were big problems," he says. "That's when I started paying attention. That's when I started asking questions: could it happen here? It's like the housing bubble and the Internet bubble. There were people around who were writing about it. It's not that there aren't people telling us that this is crazy. It's that you refuse to believe that you are crazy."

He hands me a chart. It shows that the city's pension costs when he first became interested in the subject were projected to run $73 million a year. This year they would be $245 million: pension and health costs of retired workers now are more than half the budget. In three years' time pension costs alone would come to $400 million, though "if you were to adjust for real-life expectancy it is more like six hundred fifty million dollars." Legally obliged to meet these costs, the city can respond only by cutting elsewhere. As a result, San Jose, once run by 7,450 city workers, was now being run by 5,400 city workers. The city was back to staffing levels of 1988, when it had a quarter of a million fewer residents to service. The remaining workers had taken a 10 percent pay cut; yet even that was not enough to offset the increase in the city's pension liability. The city had closed its libraries three days a week. It had cut back servicing its parks. It had refrained from opening a brand-new community center built before the housing bust, because it couldn't pay to staff the place. For the first time in history it had laid off police officers and firefighters.

By 2014, Reed had calculated, a city of a million people, the tenth largest city in the United States, would be serviced by 1,600 public workers. "There is no way to run a city with that level of staffing," he said. "You start to ask: What is a city? Why do we bother to live together? But that's just the start." The problem was going to grow worse until, as he put it, "you get to one." A single employee to service the entire city, presumably with a focus on paying pensions. "I don't know how far out you have to go until you get to one," said Reed, "but it isn't all that far." At that point, if not before, the city would be nothing more than a vehicle to pay the retirement costs of its former workers. The only clear solution was if former city workers up and died, soon. But former city workers were, blessedly, living longer than ever.

This wasn't a hypothetical scary situation, said Reed. "It's a mathematical inevitability." In spirit it reminded me of Bernard Madoff's investment business. Anyone who looked at Madoff's returns and understood them could see he was running a Ponzi scheme; only one person who had

251

understood them bothered to blow the whistle, and no one listened to him. (See *No One Would Listen: A True Financial Thriller*, by Harry Markopolos.)

In his negotiations with the unions, the mayor has gotten nowhere. "I understand the police and firefighters," he says. "They think, We're the most important, and everyone else goes [gets fired] first." The police union recently suggested to the mayor that he close the libraries for the other four days. "We looked into that," Reed says. "If you close the libraries an extra day you pay for twenty or thirty cops." Adding twenty more police officers for a year wouldn't solve anything. The cops who were spared this year would be axed next, in response to the soaring costs of the pensions of city workers who already had retired. On the other side of the inequality is the taxpayer of San Jose, who has no interest in paying more than he already does. "It's not that we're insolvent and can't pay our bills," says Reed. "It's about willingness."

I ask him what the chances were that, in this pinch, he could raise taxes. He holds up a thumb and index finger: zero. He's recently coined a phrase, he says: "service-level insolvency." Service-level insolvency means that the expensive community center that has been built and named cannot be opened. It means closing libraries three days a week. It isn't financial bankruptcy; it's cultural bankruptcy.

"How on earth did this happen?" I ask him.

"The only way I can explain it," he says, "is that they got the money because it was there." But he has another way to explain it, and in a moment he offers it up.

"I think we've suffered from a series of mass delusions," he says.

I didn't completely understand what he meant, and said so.

"We're all going to be rich," he says. "We're all going to live forever. All the forces in the state are lined up to preserve the status quo. To preserve the delusion. And here—this place—is where the reality hits."

On the way back to the elevators I chatted with two of Mayor Reed's aides. He'd mentioned to me that as bad as they might think they have it in San Jose, a lot of other American cities have it worse. "I count my blessings when I talk to the mayors of other cities," he'd said.

"Which city do you pity most?" I asked, just before the elevator doors closed.

The aides laughed and in unison said, "Vallejo!"

WELCOME TO VALLEJO, CITY OF OPPORTUNITY, reads the sign on the way in, but the shops that remain open display signs that say, WE ACCEPT FOOD STAMPS. Weeds surround abandoned businesses, and all traffic lights are set to permanently blink, which is a formality as there are no longer any cops to police the streets. Vallejo is the one city in the Bay Area where you can park anywhere and not worry about getting a ticket, because there are no meter maids, either. The windows of city hall are dark but its front porch is a hive of activity. A young man in a backwards baseball cap, sunglasses, and a new pair of Nike sneakers stands on a low wall and calls out an address:

"Nine hundred Cambridge Drive," he says. "In Benicia."

The people in the crowd below instantly begin bidding. From 2006 to 2010 the value of Vallejo real estate fell 66 percent. One in sixteen homes in the city are in foreclosure. This is apparently the fire sale, but the characters involved are so shady and furtive that I can hardly believe it. I stop to ask what's going on, but the bidders don't want to talk. "Why would I tell you anything?" says a guy sitting in a Coleman folding chair. He obviously thinks he's shrewd, and perhaps he is.

The lobby of city hall is completely empty. There's a receptionist's desk but no receptionist. Instead, there's a sign: TO FORECLOSURE AUCTIONEERS AND FORECLOSURE BIDDERS: PLEASE DO NOT CONDUCT BUSINESS IN THE CITY HALL LOBBY.

On the third floor I find the offices of the new city manager, Phil Batchelor, but when I walk in there is no one in sight. It's just a collection of empty cubicles. At length a woman appears and leads me to Batchelor himself. He's in his sixties and, oddly enough, a published author. He's written one book on how to raise children and another on how to face death. Both deliver an overtly Christian message, but he doesn't come across as evangelical; he comes across as sensible, and a little weary. His day job, before he retired, was running cities with financial difficulties. He came out of retirement to take this job, but only after the city council had asked him a few times. "The more you say no, the more determined they are to get you," he says. His chief demand was not financial but social: he'd only take the job if the people on the city council ceased being nasty to one another and behaved civilly. He actually got that in writing, and they've kept their end of the bargain. "I've been in a lot of places that have been in a lot of trouble but I've never seen anything like this," he says. He then lays out what he finds unusual, beginning with the staffing levels. He's now running the city, and he has a staff of one: I just met her. "When she goes out to the bathroom she has to lock the door," he says, "because I'm in meetings, and we have no one else."

Back in 2008, unable to come to terms with its many creditors, Vallejo had declared bankruptcy. Eighty percent of the city's budget—and the

255

lion's share of the claims that had thrown it into bankruptcy—were wrapped up in the pay and benefits of public safety workers. Relations between the police and the firefighters, on the one hand, and the citizens, on the other, were at historic lows. The public safety workers thought that the city was out to screw them on their contracts; the citizenry thought that the public safety workers were using fear as a tool to extort money from them. The local joke was that "P.D." stands for "Pay or Die." The city council meetings had become exercises in outrage: at one, a citizen arrived and tossed a severed pig's head onto the floor. "There's no good reason why Vallejo is as fucked up as it is," says a longtime resident named Marc Garman, who created a website to catalogue the civil war. "It's a boat ride to San Francisco. You throw a stone and you hit Napa." Since the bankruptcy, the police and fire departments had been cut in half; some number of the citizens who came to Phil Batchelor's office did so to say they no longer felt safe in their own homes. All other city services had been reduced effectively to zero. "Do you know that some cities actually pave their streets?" says Batchelor. "That's not here."

I notice on his shelf a copy of *Fortune* magazine, with Meredith Whitney on the cover. And as he talked about the bankrupting of Vallejo I realized that I had heard this story before, or a private-sector version of it. The people who had power in the society, and were charged with saving it from itself, had instead bled the society to death. The problem with police officers and firefighters isn't a public-sector problem; it isn't a problem with government; it's a problem with the entire society. It's what happened on Wall Street in the run-up to the subprime crisis. It's a problem of people taking what they can, just because they can, without regard to the larger social consequences. It's not just a coincidence that the debts of cities and states spun out of control at the same time as the debts of individual Americans. Alone in a dark room with a pile of money, Americans knew exactly what they wanted to do, from the top of the society to the bottom. They'd been conditioned to grab as much as they could, without thinking about the long-term consequences. Afterward, the people on Wall Street would privately bemoan the low morals of the American people who walked away from their subprime loans, and the American people would express outrage at the Wall Street people who paid themselves a fortune to design the bad loans.

Having failed to persuade its public safety workers that it could not afford to make them rich, the city of Vallejo, California, had hit bottom: it could fall no lower. "My approach has been I don't care who is to blame," Batchelor said. "We needed to change." When I met him, a few months after he had taken the job, he was still trying to resolve a narrow financial dispute: the city had 1,013 claimants with half a billion dollars in claims but only $6 million to dole out to them. They were survivors of a shipwreck on a life raft with limited provisions. His job, as he saw it, was to persuade them that the only chance of survival was to work together. He didn't view the city's main problem as financial: the financial problems were the symptom. The disease was the culture. Just a few weeks earlier, he had sent a memo to the remaining city staff—the city council, the mayor, the public safety workers. The central message was that if you want to fix this place you need to change how you behave, each and every one of you. "It's got to be about the people," he said. "Teach them respect for each other, integrity and how to strive for excellence. Cultures change. But people need to want to change. People convinced against their will are of the same opinion still."

"How do you change the culture of an entire city?" I asked him.

"First of all we look internally," he said.

THE ROAD OUT of Vallejo passes directly through the office of Dr. Peter Whybrow, a British neuroscientist at UCLA with a theory about American life. He thinks the dysfunction in

America's society is a by-product of America's success. In academic papers and a popular book, *American Mania*, Whybrow argues, in effect, that human beings are neurologically ill-designed to be modern Americans. The human brain evolved over hundreds of thousands of years in an environment defined by scarcity. It was not designed, at least originally, for an environment of extreme abundance. "Human beings are wandering around with brains that are fabulously limited," he says cheerfully. "We've got the core of the average lizard." Wrapped around this reptilian core, he explains, is a mammalian layer (associated with maternal concern and social interaction), and around that is wrapped a third layer, which enables feats of memory and the capacity for abstract thought. "The only problem," he says, "is our passions are still driven by the lizard core. We are set up to acquire as much as we can of things we perceive as scarce, particularly sex, safety, and food." Even a person on a diet who sensibly avoids coming face-to-face with a piece of chocolate cake will find it hard to control himself if the chocolate cake somehow finds him. Every pastry chef in America understands this, and now neuroscience does, too. "When faced with abundance, the brain's ancient reward pathways are difficult to suppress," says Whybrow. "In that moment the value of eating the chocolate cake exceeds the value of the diet. We cannot think down the road when we are faced with the chocolate cake."

The richest society the world has ever seen has grown rich by devising better and better ways to give people what they want. The effect on the brain of lots of instant gratification is something like the effect on the right hand of cutting off the left: the more the lizard core is used the more dominant it becomes. "What we're doing is minimizing the use of the part of the brain that lizards don't have," says Whybrow. "We've created physiological dysfunction. We have lost the ability to self-regulate, at all levels of the society. The five million dollars you get paid at Goldman Sachs if you do whatever they ask you to do—that is the chocolate cake upgraded."

The succession of financial bubbles, and the amassing of personal and public debt, Whybrow views as simply an expression of the lizard-brained way of life. A color-coded map of American personal indebtedness could be laid on top of the Centers for Disease Control's color-coded map that illustrates the fantastic rise in rates of obesity across the United States since 1985 without disturbing the general pattern. The boom in trading activity in individual stock portfolios; the spread of legalized gambling; the rise of drug and alcohol addiction; it is all of a piece. Everywhere you turn you see Americans sacrifice their long-term interests for a short-term reward.

What happens when a society loses its ability to self-regulate, and insists on sacrificing its long-term self-interest for short-term rewards? How does the story end? "We could regulate ourselves if we chose to think about it," Whybrow says. "But it does not appear that is what we are going to do." Apart from that remote possibility, Whybrow imagines two possible outcomes. The first he illustrates with a true story, which might be called the parable of the pheasant. Last spring, on sabbatical at the University of Oxford, he was surprised to discover that he was able to rent an apartment inside Blenheim Palace, the Churchill family home. The previous winter at Blenheim had been harsh, and the pheasant hunters had been efficient; as a result, just a single pheasant had survived in the palace gardens. This bird had gained total control of a newly seeded field. Its intake of food, normally regulated by its environment, was now entirely unregulated: it could eat all it wanted, and it did. The pheasant grew so large that when other birds challenged it for seed, it would simply frighten them away. The fat pheasant became a tourist attraction and even acquired a name: Henry. "Henry was the biggest pheasant anyone had ever seen," says Whybrow. "Even after he got fat, he just ate and ate." It didn't take long before Henry was obese. He could still eat as much as he wanted, but he could no longer fly. Then one day he was gone: a fox ate him.

The other possible outcome was only slightly more hopeful: to hit bottom. To realize what has happened to us, because we have no other choice. "If we refuse to regulate ourselves, the only regulators are our environment," says Whybrow, "and the way that environment deprives us." For meaningful change to occur, in other words, we need the environment to administer the necessary level of pain.

IN AUGUST 2011, the same week that Standard & Poor's downgraded the debt of the United States government, a judge approved the bankruptcy plan for Vallejo, California. Vallejo's creditors ended up with five cents on the dollar, public employees with something like twenty and thirty cents on the dollar. The city no longer received any rating at all from Moody's and Standard & Poor's. It would take years to build the track record needed to obtain a decent rating. The absence of a rating mattered little, as the last thing the city needed to do was to go out and borrow money from strangers.

More out of idle curiosity than with any clear purpose, I drove up again to Vallejo and paid a call on the fire department. In the decay of our sense of common purpose, the firefighters are a telling sign that we are approaching a new bottom. It isn't hard to imagine how a police department might wind up in conflict with the community it's hired to protect. A person who becomes a police officer enjoys the authority. He wants to stop the bad guys. He doesn't necessarily need to care for the people he polices. A person who becomes a firefighter wants to be a good guy. He wants to be *loved*.

The Vallejo firefighter I met with that morning was named Paige Meyer. He was forty-one years old. He had short salt-and-pepper hair and olive skin, with traces of burn marks on his cheeks. His natural expression was a smile. He wasn't particularly either religious or political. ("I'm not necessarily a God guy.") The closest thing he had to a religion, apart from his family, was his job. He was extremely proud of it, and of his colleagues. "I don't want this to sound arrogant at all," he said. "But many departments in nicer communities, they get a serious fire maybe once a year. We get them all the time." The Vallejo population is older and poorer than in many surrounding cities, and older still are the buildings it lives in. The typical Vallejo house is a charming, highly inflammable wooden Victorian. "In this town we fight fires," says Meyer. "This town *rips*." The department was shaped by its environment: they were extremely aggressive firefighters. "When I came to this department you *rolled* to a fire," he said. "You were not going to see an exterior water stream from this department. We're going in. You have some knucklehead calling in with a sore throat— your giddyup is not so fast. But I'll tell you something about this department. They get a call that there's a baby choking or a ten-year-old not breathing, you better get out of the way, or you're going to get run over."

As a young man, to pay his way through college, Meyer had worked as a state beach lifeguard at lakes in central California. He assumed that there would be little drama in the work but people would turn up, get drunk, and attempt to drown. A few of the times he pulled people from the water, they were in bad enough shape that they needed paramedics; the fire department was there on the spot. He started talking to firefighters and found that "they all absolutely loved what they did. You get to go and *live* and create a second family. How can you not like that?" He came to Vallejo in 1998, at the age of twenty-eight. He had left a cushy job in Sunnyvale, outside San Jose, where there aren't many fires, precisely because he wanted to fight fires. "In other departments," he says, "I wasn't a firefighter. The first six months of the job here, I was out at two in the morning at a fire every other week. I couldn't believe it." The houses of Vallejo are mainly balloon-frame construction.

The interior walls have no firebreaks: from bottom to top, all four walls carry fire as efficiently as a chimney. One of the rookie mistakes in Vallejo is to put the fire out on the ground floor, only to look up and see it roaring out of the roof. "When we get to a fire we say, 'Boom! Send someone up to the attic.' Because the fire is going right to the attic."

Meyer actually had made that rookie mistake. One day not long after he'd arrived, he'd jumped off the truck already breathing air from a tank and raced into what appeared to be a burning one-bedroom apartment. He knocked down the door and put the attack line on the fire and then wondered why the fire wasn't going out. "It should have been getting cooler, but it was getting hotter and hotter." Right in front of his face, on his plastic mask, lines trickled down, like rain on a windshield. The old-school firefighters left their ears exposed so they could feel the heat: the heat contained the critical information. Meyer could only see the heat: his helmet was melting. "If your helmet starts to shrivel up and melt, that's not cool," he says. A melting helmet, among the other problems it presents, is an indication that a room is about to flash. Flashing, he explains, "is when all combustible materials simultaneously ignite. You're a baked potato after that." He needed more water, or to get out; but his ego was invested in staying inside, and so he stayed inside. Moments later a backup arrived, with another, bigger hose.

Afterward, he understood his mistake: the building was three stories, built on a slope that disguised its size, and the fire had reached the attic. "I'm not saying that if the backup hadn't come when it did I'd be dead," he says, but that's exactly what he is saying. The scar on his face is from that fire. "I needed to learn to control my environment," he said. "I'd had this false sense of security."

When you take care of something you become attached to it, and he'd become attached to Vallejo. He was extremely uncomfortable with conflict between his union and the citizens, and had found himself in screaming matches with the union's negotiator. Meyer thought firefighters, who tended to be idealistic and trusting, were easily duped. He further thought the rank-and-file had been deceived both by the city, which lied to them repeatedly in negotiations, and by their own leadership, which harnessed the firefighters' outrage to make unreasonable demands in the union-negotiated contract with the city. What was lost at the bargaining table was the reason they did what they did for a living. "I'm telling you," Meyer says, "when I started, I didn't know what I was getting paid. I didn't care what I was getting paid. I didn't know about benefits. A lot of things that we're politicizing today were not even in my mind. I was just thinking of my dream job. Let me tell you something else: nobody cared in 2007 how much I made. If I made six figures they said, 'Shit, man, you deserve it. You ran into a burning building.' Because everyone had a job. All they knew about our job is that it was dangerous. The minute the economy started to collapse, people started looking at each other."

Today the backup that may or may not have saved him is far less likely to arrive. When Vallejo entered bankruptcy, the fire department was cut from 121 to 67, for a city of 112,000 people. The department handles roughly 13,000 calls a year, extremely high for the population. When people feel threatened or worried by anything except other people, they call the fire department. Most of these calls are of the cat-in-the-tree variety—pointless. ("You never see the skeleton of a cat in a tree.") They get calls from people who have headaches. They get calls from people who have itches where they can't scratch. They have to answer every call. ("The best call I ever had was phantom leg pain in a guy with no legs.") To deal with these huge numbers of calls, they once had eight stations, eight three-person engine companies, a four-man truck company (used only for actual fires and rescue calls), one fireboat, one confined space rescue team, and a team to deal with hazardous materials. They now are down to four stations, four engines, and a truck.

This is particularly relevant to Paige Meyer because, two months ago, he became Vallejo's new fire chief. It surprised him: he hadn't even applied for the job. The city manager, Phil Batchelor, just called him to his office one day. "He didn't ever really ask me if I wanted the job," says Meyer. "He just asked how's the family, told me he was giving me the job, and asked if I had any problem with that."

He didn't, actually. He sat down and made a list of ways to improve the department. He faced a fresh challenge: how to deliver service that was the same as before, or even better than before, with half the resources. How to cope with an environment of scarcity. He began to measure things that hadn't been measured. The number one cause of death in firefighting was heart attacks. Number two was a truck crash. He was now in charge of a department that would be both overworked and in a hurry. Fewer people doing twice the work probably meant twice the number of injuries per firefighter. He'd decided to tailor fitness regimens to fit the job. With fewer fire stations and fewer firefighters in them, the response times were going to be slower. He'd need to find new ways to speed things up. A longer response time meant less room for error; a longer response time meant the fires they'd be fighting would be bigger. He had some thoughts about the most efficient way to fight these bigger fires. He began, in short, to rethink firefighting.

When people pile up debts they will find difficult and perhaps even impossible to repay, they are saying several things at once. They are obviously saying that they want more than they can immediately afford. They are saying, less obviously, that their present wants are so important that, to satisfy them, it is worth some future difficulty. But in making that bargain they are implying that when the future difficulty arrives, they'll figure it out. They don't always do that. But you can never rule out the possibility that they will. As idiotic as optimism can sometimes seem, it has a weird habit of paying off.

# ACKNOWLEDGMENTS

At the end of every book I write there always seem to be people who deserve more than to be thanked at the end of a book. This one is no different. Act II of the financial crisis was set in places it would never have occurred to me to go. I'd like to thank Graydon Carter and Doug Stumpf, at *Vanity Fair*, for encouraging me to go there, and Jaime Lalinde, for researching these places so well that I sometimes felt he, not I, should be writing about them. Theo Phanos offered me not only friendship and encouragement but the shrewd views of an interesting money manager, from start to finish. At W. W. Norton, Janet Byrne has appeared from nowhere to improve my prose and, to the extent it is possible for an editor to do this, save me from myself. Starling Lawrence remains my touchstone.

**Center Point Publishing**
600 Brooks Road ● PO Box 1
Thorndike ME 04986-0001 USA

**(207) 568-3717**

**US & Canada:
1 800 929-9108**
www.centerpointlargeprint.com